MW01240695

DEDICATION

Dedicated with love to my mother Maggie (Late) and my family Bridget,Lindelani,Uhone and my sister Martha for the love they give and more important, the love they receive

My church,relatives,friends,my community, my country and my world you are awesome!!!!

World Class Trading Secrets® Graduates and Students you guys are Magnificent!!!!!!

Millionaire Pillars Team, Events Fans and Audience, You folks Rocks.........

Success Resources (World Leading Events Company) I am glad I did,your patience and professionalism are just a couple of traits I admire for the rest of my life.

To My mentors And Gurus out there, to mention just a few T.Harv Eker, Greg Secker, Tony Robbins, Richard Branson, Robert Kiyosaki,Dr John Demartini, Les Brown, Nick Vujicic you have helped me to reprogram my mind and dream bigger. It boiled down to this: the only things that will change you from where you are currently to where you want to be in two,three,five or twenty years from now are the quantity,quality of the books you read and implement what you have read immediately. I hope this Forex Trading Strategies and Bonus 6 Figure Life Lessons helps you to accomplish your goals.

" I live by a philosophy and I am also guided by the power of my associations." Titus Maduwa

"What you focus on expands." T.Harv Eker.

One man's ceiling is another man's floor." Paul Simon

You've got to learn how to fall, before you learn to fly." Paul Simon

The Power of Forex Trading Strategies & Bonus 6 Figure Life Lessons

It boiled down to this:

The story of Chinese Bamboo Tree

Like any plant, growth of the Chinese Bamboo Tree requires nurturing through water, fertile soil, and sunshine.

In its first year though, we see no visible signs of growth in spite of providing all of these things.

In the second year (again), there is no growth above soil.

The third, fourth year....still show no signs of anything happening.

Our patience is tested, and we begin to wonder if our efforts caring for and watering the tree will ever be rewarded. We start to doubt ourselves and question the value of our efforts. Inevitably, we contemplate quitting.

But then finally in the fifth year something amazing happens.....

The Chinese Bamboo Tree grows 80 to 90 feet tall in just six weeks!

But think for a moment, does the Chinese Bamboo Tree really grow 80 to 90 feet in six weeks? Did the Chinese Bamboo Tree lie dormant for four years only to grow exponentially in the fifth?

Or, was the little tree growing underground, developing a root system strong enough to support its potential for outward growth in the fifth year and beyond?

The answer is (of course) obvious. Had the tree not developed a strong unseen foundation it could not have sustained its life as it grew. The same principle is true for people.

People, who patiently toil towards worthwhile dreams and goals, building strong character while overcoming adversity and challenge, grow the strong internal foundation to handle success. Meanwhile get-rich-quickers and lottery winners usually are unable to sustain unearned sudden wealth. They haven't become the person they need to be to support such success.

And the Chinese Bamboo Tree farmer dug up his little seed every year to see if it was growing, he would have stunted the tree's growth. In other words, the actions caused by self-doubt would've halted the miracle from ever taking shape and cause him to go backwards.
You have to keep fighting. As Zig Ziglar said you have to keep pumping!

Success is always slower than we want but it's worth it. The only questions are how bad do you want it? And how long are you willing to work for it?

Table of Contents

Fill in the blank..

Your Biggest WHY for Trading...

Forex Trading Strategies
How to Be a Super Successful Forex Trader

In Case We haven't Met Yet.........

I am Titus Maduwa Founder of Millionaire Pillars™ as well as the Creator of World Class Trading Secrets® System that helps beginners, busy professionals to create additional source of income and to assist those who feel overwhelmed and unable to balance career with actually having a life, to excel in their day to day professional lives while enjoying their free time with family and friends.

What is Forex Trading?

"You can never cross the ocean until you have the courage to lose sight of the shore." ~ Christopher Columbus

Our World Class Trading Secrets® involves dealing in international currencies. Here, you can sell currency of one country to buy that of another. The trader deals in Foreign Exchange [Forex] at the most appropriate time to profit from the transaction. Good ability to forecast plays a vital role here. One may wonder how Forex trading can be such a lucrative earning opportunity since fluctuations in exchange is so little.

But remember, when done in big volumes, a minor change can mean a lot. There are many non-monetary advantages to it as well. Anyone who wants to deal in Forex can do so, since only the basic knowledge is required for it. Don't stress you are all covered.

World Class Trading Secrets® will help you earn a lot of money. But there are certain conditions to follow before trading in Forex. Firstly, one must have a thorough knowledge about the trends in the stock market, the basics of trading and risk-taking ability. You will get all the help you need for attaining these conditions very easily from us.

There are many sites on the internet which can help you clarify your basics and help you brave rough weather. A good reason why Forex trading can be considered is the fact that there are frequent fluctuations in currencies, though in percentage terms it may be small.

You gain if the fluctuation favors you and the reverse holds true as well. No one can accurately predict the trend of the currencies. Liquidity is another reason why Forex trading is so popular.

Now the most important part – in Forex, you can make huge sums of money even if your initial investment is on a lower side. You can invest as little as $50,000. Rich people have no upper cap to the amount of investment. So remember that even with a nominal investment, the earning ability is undoubtedly very huge.

Most of the great businesses are connected to the world of internet today, and Forex trading is no exception. You can deal in foreign currencies right from your home. In fact, it is fully conducted online. You have the liberty to choose when you want to trade, and you don't need to meet any deadlines.

Basically, you can be your own boss. The process of online trading is fairly simple for anyone to understand. At World Class Trading Secrets® we help people to open an account for Forex trading and our dedicated team will complete the rest of the formalities. The only bit you need to do is get ready with your investment amount.

So, it is thus clear that Forex trading can be one of the best businesses to earn money. Though there is a level of risk attached to it, but it can be avoided with due care and an alert mind!

Importance of Forex trading

"Winning isn't everything, but wanting to win is." ~ Vince Lombardi

Foreign Exchange [Forex] involves exchanging of different foreign currencies for a profit. The reason for buying the currency of another country may be the need to buy some commodity of the said country as well, besides making money through the difference in exchange rates.

In the latter case, people buy currency of a foreign country when the rate in the market is low, and sell it off when the rates go up. Currency trading is usually done between the central banks, the government, speculators and MNCs. Nations cannot trade with each other without the presence of a foreign market.

A huge amount of money is daily traded in the Forex market, though the amount invested by an individual trader may be very low. No one individually can have any influence on the Forex fluctuations, not even the government. So it can easily be concluded that the level of the currency reflects the strength or the weakness of the economy of a country. So this makes the Forex market a good place for competition.

The government and the central bank do try to stabilize the currency of their country by speculating, by buying and selling currencies at appropriate times. So they can influence the market if they conduct a trade in huge volumes, though. To buy its own currency, however, the government or the central bank must have huge reserves of foreign currency with them. So it is virtually impossible to inflate the currency value artificially.

Banks trade a lot in foreign currencies and this forms a chunk of the volume in the Forex market. They buy currencies not only as individual bodies, but also on behalf of their clients. They trade in lots of futures. Till a few years back, the brokers could influence the volumes of trading in the Forex market. But due to the electronic services available now, the services of brokers is not required. It's easy to operate electronically.

Trading with international countries is possible only with the existence of Forex markets. When there is no Forex market, there is no common currency between two countries, so one cannot evaluate the value of one currency with respect to the other.

The buyer pays the seller in the former's currency. With the money so received, the seller buys goods in the buyer's country and sells those goods in his [seller] country.

Only then he is able to know how much he has earned through the export. In the presence of a Forex market, though, it is very easy for a seller to know of his earnings at the very instant that he conducts an export trade. In the same manner, the buyer too will have a thorough knowledge of the cost he will have to incur to buy goods from an international country.

Four Main Types of Orders in Forex Market

"Twenty years from now you will be more disappointed by the things that you didn't do than by the ones you did do, so throw off the bowlines, sail away from safe harbor, catch the trade winds in your sails. Explore, Dream, Discover." ~ Mark Twain

There are many kinds of orders which traders can place to transact in the Forex market, for making profit out of it.

- **Market Order**
  The market order is the most simple and common kind or order. Here, the trader buys and sells the currency at the rate prevailing in the market at the time of placing the order. Due to the huge size of the market and the high volatility, trends can reverse any instant, so people prefer placing orders at the market price to guard themselves against any adverse trend.

- **Limit order**
  In this case, the trader specifies a price at which he may wish to buy or sell the currency. Suppose a trader has bought GBP against the USD at 1.9710, then he can place a sell order at 1.9725, when the exchange will execute the order and he will profit from it. The order will get cancelled if the target price is not achieved during the day.

- **Stop loss order**
  Due to the volatility, stop losses are essential. They determine the maximum loss a trader is willing to suffer. Suppose in the above instance, the risk-taking ability of the trader is low, then he may place a stop loss at 1.9705, at which level the exchange will book losses for him, and he won't be affected by any fall below 1.9705.

- **Entry order**
  Such an order is filled only when certain conditions are met in the market, which the order specifies. The entry order can be a limit entry order or even a stop entry order.

  - **Limit entry order**
  As an example, let's assume that the current market price for GBP/USD is 1.9705-10. This implies that the trader can transact at these levels. Here, a trader can put a limit entry order to sell his holdings at a price more than the market price, say, 1.9715. His order would be executed only if that price is attained. In the similar manner, he can place an order for buying at a level of, say 1.9700, and his 'buy' order would remain pending till the price falls to that level.

- **Stop entry order**

Such an order is generally used when the trader has sufficient grounds to believe that the currency is trading in a fixed range and believes that it is on the verge of a breakout from that range. He might want to buy at a price higher than the market price or sell at a lower price than the market price. In the same example, the trader may go ahead and buy at 1.9720 or sell at 1.9690, where he believes that once these levels are attained, the currency will only go up or fall further, as the case may be. A trader exercises the stop entry order only when a trader has reasonable grounds to believe that there will be sharp movements in the currency rates in the Forex market.

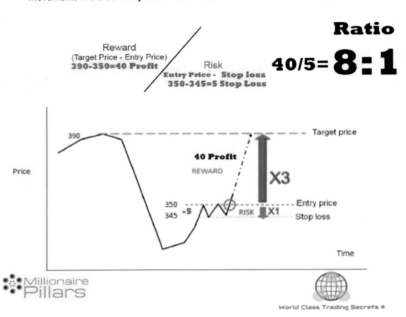

Forex Trading Price Movements- How and Why Markets Move and How to Profit

"We become what we think about." ~ Earl Nightingale

Understanding expense trends of Forex is not easy at all. Businessmen often get wrong ideas and make agendas based on them and suffer losses. The following can help you understand the trends:

You predict the Forex expense trends

Businessmen observe a certain level and jumps on to it thinking that it's stable. However, this is simply based on assumption and that never works in Forex business. There is no accurate prediction.

If wining is the goal, you have to base the business on the sure shot expense trends. Related to this, there are certain factors given below.

The Market obeys Scientific Laws

There is a notion, which believes that market trends are based on logic. Some believers are Gann, Elliot and the followers of Fibonacci.

However, if everybody knew everything, prices would never have been a surprise and markets would be non-existent. The layman would accept these ideas and their fantastic suggestions. However facts say otherwise.

Business Can be made of News

It is not advisable as news is actually insignificant. The way news is supposed is what decides the movements. Let's see how trends occur.

Actual Expense Trends

Basics + Individual Insight into them = Forex Market Trends

People are seldom rational. They often function emotionally, which is why logical reasoning does not always hold true. The real human psychology is consistent but these matters have no logic:

1. People make costs move to extreme and these passing points can be used profitably.
2. Carry on with business. Don't get into guessing. And don't gamble.

Win the Competition

Forex is a sport and competition is based on chances. You may not be able to determine chances but you will never lose.

That applies not for every instance but try out on big probability situations and you will surely take the cake with very few losses. Get huge proceeds in due course of time.
Voracity and panic fluctuate costs, creating points that are visible on Forex schedules and can be used gainfully.

It's a game so when prices fluctuate on your side, get to business. Control your finances well and be a winner.

Be Imperfect but Never a Loser

Forex markets teem with those who attempt guessing and try to get a non-existent undisclosed trend cipher. Even though Forex expense trends seem disordered, basing your business on cost fluctuations will make you a winner.

It may not be an ideal business for many, however if done right, you can make a lot of money through forex trading.

Forex Traders: The Need to Be Objective

"When it feels like you're about to fall, it might be you're about to fly." ~ Dr. Denise Barrett

It is difficult for Forex traders to realize that the currency market is extremely unpredictable. As new traders spend a long time trying to learn the mechanics of the foreign exchange trade and focus their time and energy on trying to find a method for predicting movements, they naturally expect there to be rules governing the movement of the market. This not being the case, many traders find themselves at a disadvantage.

While Forex traders have a number of tools at their disposal, which allow them to judge the right time to open or close a position, many prefer to rely mostly on one tool. So, having opened a position, they watch their favorite indicator and, to a large extent, base their trading decisions solely on it, ignoring the others.

This works well enough until that indicator starts telling them something different from what the others are. Traders caught in an open position which their favorite tool is telling them to hold, will often do so, despite the fact that other tools are telling them to close and get off the market, and end up losing money.

The basic problem, of course, is that the trader is not looking at the market as is, but through the lenses of his own expectations about it and further using his favorite indicator to reinforce those ideas instead of looking at the bigger picture. And, encouraged by the fact that his chosen indicator is forecasting the profit he wants, the trader is focusing more on money than on the market.

If the Forex market was not unpredictable, it would collapse because all traders would profit all the time. There are many tools that can help traders predict the direction of the market and they usually do an efficient job. But even in the hands of the most experienced traders, the best tools occasionally fail to predict the market's movements correctly.

Losing in trade because of predicting the market wrongly is an innate part of Forex trading and traders need to accept it. Besides, they need to learn to avoid getting in a position where they do not have many choices.

For this, the trader needs to accept the fact that the foreign exchange market pretty much has a mind of its own and the traders have to follow its movements instead of trying to make it go in the direction they want it to.

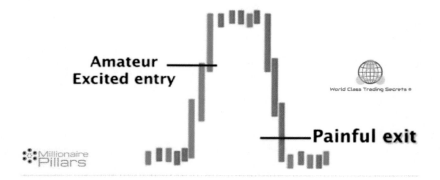

Forex Trading Tools

There is no one single super smart Forex trading tool which gives you profit, profit and more profit. The only possible solution is to use a combination of different tools to identify the favorable market forces to get a maximum number of high probability trades over a period of time. Trendlines are the most popular and reliable Forex trading tool which many successful traders give their testimonial for.

The Three Trend line Strategy

Trend Lines are an important tool for trend identification and confirmation in technical analysis. It is a straight line that connects two or more price points and then extends into the future to guide you.

There will be lines drawn across significant lows in an uptrend, and significant highs in a downtrend. To roughly classify trend lines, we can divide them into three as short term trendlines, medium term trendlines and long term trendlines.

1. **Short Term Trendlines**
   Draw these lines across the most recent two lows for an uptrend or across most recent two highs for a downtrend. Best observations are found on a smaller time frame such as a 15 minute or 30 minute chart.

2. **Medium Term Trendlines**
   These are best observed on a higher time frame like a 60 minute chart. It either connects the nearest significant low to current price action to the previous significant low in an uptrend or the nearest significant high to current price action to the previous significant high in a downtrend.

3. **Long Term Trendlines**
   It uses higher time frames such as the 4 hour chart or the daily chart to draw long term trendlines using the same method of Medium Term Trendlines. The long term trend line is considered as an effective Forex trading tool. The daily chart is used mostly by traders of big institutions who do not usually engage in small moves on an intra day level.

By drawing a trend line on a daily chart you can graphically analyze where price is and where it is likely to bounce. But employ trendlines as a Forex trading tool with caution and discretion. Covering your charts with every trend line possible will result in confusion and blurry analysis.

It is not a good idea to rely completely on a short time trend line. They merely give you a defined picture of current price action. These are broken often during the course of a day. Their main use is to give you a clear, instantly recognizable graphical representation of current price behavior.

If you notice price coming back to test a trend line on the higher time frames, look at other factors. Draw in horizontal lines to mark key support and resistance using previous highs and lows. Draw Fibonacci retracement and extension levels. Calculate the daily pivot points and put them on your chart. Have the 200 EMA (Exponential Moving Average) shown on your charts.

By definition of support and resistance, the sequence of highs and low cannot persist at the level of support and resistance. However, we can still look for signs that the trend is intact.

- For an uptrend, we continue to see a sequence of higher lows.
- For a downtrend, we continue to see a sequence of lower highs.

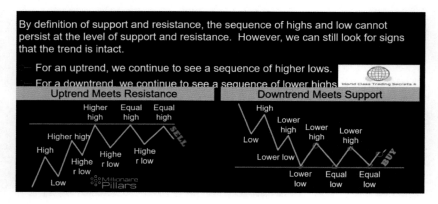

How to Win with Forex: The Step-by-Step Secrets®

"A boxer makes an impact, a dentist makes an impression and a builder creates an inspiration. Whether you make an impact, an impression or create inspiration, do something that makes a difference in someone else's life."~ Byron Reaney

When 95% of traders lose money, what makes you think you can win? To see your chances of succeeding as a forex trader, here is a checklist for you to see and become one of the elite traders, who make tremendous long term profits.

Following are a few ways to lose money. You may wish to change your mind immediately if you are thinking of trying any of them. Do this to avoid losses and continue your forex education!

1. Following a Forex Robot with Simulated Gains - You can apparently achieve success without any effort as promised by these. You are asked to accept their track records simulated going backwards. Your equity will get destroyed by trying them.

2. Day trading and Scalping - Due to the random short term volatility, simply doesn't work. Like the robots, even people selling these always have simulated track records.

Many more of these all fall into the category of trying to find someone else to give you success. This does not work in forex markets.

Apart from needing a trading edge, you also have to understand ways and reasons of it leading you to success. Let's look at this in detail.

Success Comes From Within (Belief)

The combination of a simple robust helping you to understand and trade with discipline is what forex trading is about.

You need to know what you are doing to trade with discipline. This translates into having confidence, which you definitely don't get from someone telling you what to do. You get confidence by from your own knowledge and coaching sessions.

Discipline & Losses

As you have to keep executing trading signals through losing periods, discipline is hard. This has to be continued till you hit a home run, even when the market is fooling you and taking your money.

A Trading Edge

What separates out your forex trading system from the 95% losers is your trading edge. You can answer what is your trading edge and how will it help you beat the majority. You don't have one if you don't know what it is.

Few succeed in the simple looking forex trading. These elements are present in the winners' forex trading strategy:

Using simple robust forex trading system

- Having solid grounding in the basics of forex trading

- Knowing exactly why their system will lead them to success

- Having confidence and discipline to stick with their plan

- Knowing only they are responsible for their Forex trading success

You have to stand alone, be confident of your actions and be disciplined to follow your plan in forex trading.

Success is in YOUR Hands

Sounds simple, however it is actually depends on your approach to forex trading - with the right mindset and getting right education. The trader beats himself, rather than the market beating the trader in forex trading.

Learn the basic fundamentals, get a suitable system, become confident, get an edge and be disciplined. Do all of these to enjoy currency trading success.

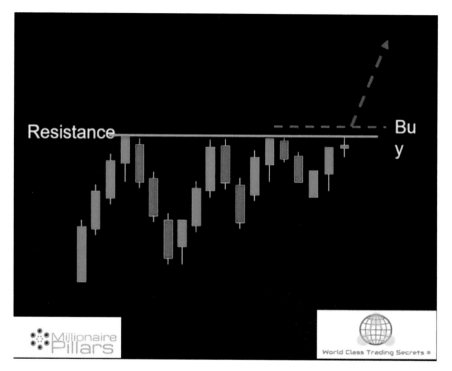

Dangers of Getting Emotional About Forex Trade

"The cool thing about being yourself is that you have no competition." ~ Yvonne Powrie

Getting emotional in the stock market is the worst thing that can happen to investors. The same goes for Forex traders as well. Seeing paper losses in everyday trade is pretty common.

Once to take a decision to buy something and make losses, you still hold on even if situations turn from bad to worse, only because you feel that things might turn back in your favor once again. The main problem here is that, the decision to stick to a losing trade for a long time is an emotional one, since you are in no mood to accept a loss and get out of the trade.

Forex market is largely influenced by the general market and you must always trade on what the indications based on the market are, and not just initiate one since your heart tells you to. At times, you might be so emotionally attached to a given currency in the Forex market, that most of your exposure to the Forex market would be in that particular currency.

Nothing wrong with it, as if you have reasonable grounds to believe that the currency will do well, then you will actually profit from the exchange. The 'wrong' thing is opening up a trade in a currency just because your heart tells you to.

In the case, if you strongly feel about any given currency, then it's better to check the reality by having the look at what the market is indicating. That will give you a clear picture of whether or not you should trade in that currency.

The basic thing that is needed to be remembered is that once you have initiated a trade, and are incurring paper losses, and by all indications, things are likely to get even worse for you, then it is much better to book losses and come out of it rather than sticking to it till a time you ultimately are able to see some gains from it. Remember, the markets have little room for emotions.

Forex trading is not a win-win situation. Be prepared to lose on some trades as well. That's the precise manner in which the market works. It is not really a question of whether you are right or not, the fact remains that markets move in an unexpected way and they have a knick of surprising people when they least expect it. All the fundamentals and even experience may be thrown into the air when the markets decide to do something.

So just follow the indications that the market gives you. If you feel that after initiating a trade, things are not going the way you had foreseen, book your losses and get out of it. You can invest the amount in some other trade and make good gains rather than sticking to your losing trade.

Trading Know How...

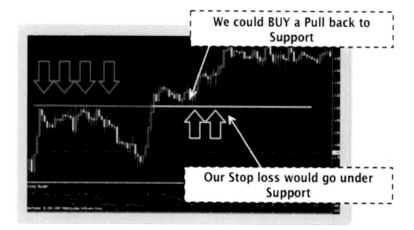

Forex Trading Strategy - Channel Breakout

"He who learns by doing, seeing done or visualizing being done understands, retains and can describe better and effectively what he learns than he who learns by simply listening and reading passively." ~ Mithra Dulloo

Forex system happens to be the greatest global trade. It taps into some movements for businessmen to gain well. One accepted Forex business agenda utilized rather gainfully in the business is called Channel Breakout.

Forex Trading Channels – Channels consist of paths made on a schedule to trace the array where exchange had been transacted in a time span. They can be simply constructed. Observe the schedule in a time span and draw lines linking the comparatively tall spot business expenses, and down under linking a comparative low spot business expenses. This will give you a picture of the business array existent during a time span like, six months.

Channel Breakout – Once the value of exchange goes up the peak network line, there is a rising network getaway. Also, once the value goes down below the lowest network spot, you get a downward network getaway. Network getaways happen upwards and downwards. With enough Forex input with scientific scrutiny, everyone may utilize the process for getting a gainful exchange business agenda.

You have to build the channels very carefully. Every meeting of lines doesn't indicate a proper getaway. If there is any fallacy in the line construction, what you observe is business out of the array, which just leads you back inside. Therefore, before anything else, gain enough knowledge on Forex.

Gainful Control of Forex channels – When you figure out the working of networks, gains will happen. Construct the business with enough pauses. Then, in case of an incorrect getaway sign, you will get tolerable losses or if luck favors you, a very low profit.

But if you are on the correct side of a proper network getaway, the tiny lack you received will be moved away and you get a good big satisfactory gain.

Any proper Forex business shareholder worth his name capitalizes on channel breakouts. In case you want to cash in the exchange markets, take out a certain amount of time for a Forex education to build this agenda and various technological scrutiny processes.

That will build up the exchange agendas, which would yield gainful consequences. If you don't give some time to completely figure out the stakes and yields contained in a Forex business agenda, you may not get the desirable consequences. So you see, your gain just depends on you.

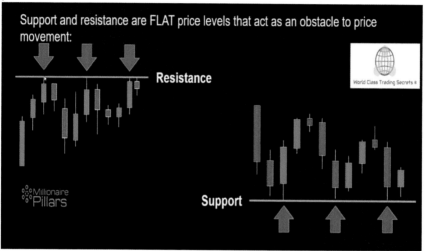

Forex Assassin vs. Forex Power Strategy

"Let's work it out with a head and heart connection." ~ Sharon Reid

For those who have an interest in the huge 3 trillion dollars a day foreign exchange market it is common knowledge that to be able to remain on the right side of the Forex market what you require is to constantly discover new plans to minimize your losses and to maximize your profits, and to always adapt so that you can grab any and every opportunity to get a bigger share of the pie.

The Forex Assassin formula and the Forex Power Strategy course are two of the most widely used currency trading tools. Both these tools have received great reviews, but their operating principles are entirely different. As a Forex trader, how would you understand which is the better tool for you? To help you out of your confusion, just read on.

The Forex Assassin formula is designed as a solution to the busy man's problems with forex trading. This tool is ideal for the average 9 to 5 professional who wishes to generate some extra income through Forex dealings but can't muster the time to either monitor the markets throughout the day or study intricate technical formulas, analysis and graphs.

Forex Assassin is a simple and convenient strategy that can be used with little or no understanding of how the market actually works. It normally takes about a quarter of an hour every week to prepare and assign a trading strategy, after which you just have to relax and allow the market to do its work.

It is very straightforward, but on the flip side also rather limited, as you are not required to have much understanding of the market. The whole target is to allow the dummy to make limited money by minimizing his chances of loss, which however is not certainly the best way to make the most money.

Conversely, the Forex Power Strategy tool offers a detailed and an in depth course in the dynamics and economics of the market. It takes into account a whole lot of material, and includes all levels of trading. As a result it requires a high investment of your time and attention to make the most of the course and absorb its lessons. So unless you can commit quite some time to it, the Forex Power Strategy tool is not quite for you.

But in return you have the assurance that by the time you complete the World Class Trading Secrets® coaching sessions, you will have achieved a better and sounder knowledge of how the market works, and thus your earning potential will be correspondingly higher.

But no matter which tool you choose, using either is better than trading just blindly in the market and ending up with huge losses.

WCTS TRADING SCHEDULES

	Monday	Tuesday	Wednesday	Thursday	Friday
Evening	FREE TIME / TRADE	FREE TIME / TRADE	FREE TIME / TRADE	FREE TIME / TRADE	FREE TIME / TRADE
Lunch	NORMAL WORK	NORMAL WORK	NORMAL WORK	NORMAL WORK	NORMAL WORK
Morning					

Millionaire Pillars

World Class Trading Secrets ®

The Correct Timing in Forex Trading

"When you look at someone as a Gift from God, you soul speaks to that person."~ Cris Raducu

When you sense a trading opportunity, the deciding factor is to know exactly when to buy. Unfortunately this is the very point at which most loose the plot by timing their entry levels improperly. But here are some basic guidelines to help you at those crucial moments:

Making Proper Use of Support and Resistance

If you try and use the fundamental rule of the share market – "buy low, sell high" – in Forex trading, you'll actually lose money. To understand you need to know how the system of support and resistance works.

A support price is a historically tested price at which traders intervene and buy, so as to "support the market". The more times this price is tested, the more bankable the support price will be. Inversely, a resistance level is defined as a level at which "prices were resisted from moving any higher". Here too the more times this level is tested, the more reliable it becomes.

Why Buy Low and Sell High Doesn't Work

The reason why this traditional wisdom is counterproductive in Forex trading is that if you actually wait for prices to fall, you're going to end up missing some of the best opportunities for making money. Consider: when a currency starts to pick up, what are the chances of its pulling back?

What if it doesn't and steadies out? If you keep waiting for a pullback, you could end up never getting in on the trade because most of the changes in currencies occur from new market highs and without any pullback.

So if you plan to focus your Forex trade strategy on waiting for an entry at support prices, wake up! You stand to loose out on the most profitable trades. What your Forex trading strategy should target is rather, to "buy high and sell higher" – i.e. you should try and do quite the reverse of what the general crowd is doing. Try and keep a lookout for any breakthroughs in support and resistance, and then sell and buy correspondingly.

It Takes Guts - But It Makes Money

The policy of going against the crowd takes courage to practice. But think over the strategy with a cool head and you shall find it is the most logical thing to do. How often have you heard of traders buying into support, but the market continuing its freefall, breaking the support?

And again, haven't you heard tell of the price continuing to soar and never getting to support, thereby making the trader miss the chance to capitalize on the trend?

So rather than be traditional and lose money, it is easier to adopt the breakouts policy: you won't be comfortable on entry but you will be making money. The trick is to break away from the pattern that the losing majority sets and to do what is productive and logical considering the common and predictable response.

The Importance of Real Time Forex Charting

"A good leader can show you greatness, but a good client can achieve the impossible."
~ Karli Brack

Do you want to earn money in the arena of foreign exchange? In order to accomplish so, you should possess in-depth technical knowledge, focused on the capability of tracking currency exchange rates, through interpreting actual forex charts.

If you are an amateur in this field, you should quickly discover authentic forex charts from the Internet or may opt for free actual forex charts. The best option is however, to take the help of free chart recognition software and mastering on it, you are well suited for this business.

Online forex charts keep you updated about currency values at any time, even between short time gaps like minutes to long intervals like several years. The graphs depicting the oscillations in rates are line graphs, or bar diagrams or candlestick charts.

Line charts are easy to interpret and help you to broadly check ups and downs of prices. It aids you to track the current trend of rate movement. On the contrary, bar charts are not as lucid as line graphs but supply a much in depth information.

To summarize, the length of a bar chart depicts the amount of rise or fall in price and the breadth gives the duration, which has witnessed this. Initial and final rates are mentioned on chart so that you can identify the range and whether it's a fall or rise. There are pattern recognition software available that interpret the bar diagrams for you and make your task easier.

The Japanese were first found to use candlestick charts to plot their amount of their rice production. Since then they have been increasingly popular. Though they are similar to bar diagrams, they are colored.

Each color acts as a code to signify the rise or fall in price. The index is written on the graph itself. Thus candlestick plots are much more user friendly than bars. Candlestick charts have unique patterns and they are as pretty as to be named after natural beauties. As soon as you are able to identify the particular pattern you will identify the market trend.

An actual forex chart is often complemented with many technical indicators such as trend, strength, volatility and cyclic movements. A forex chart is useful itself, but this adjunct information is provided to ease your task of market analysis to predict both movements in the market and market volume.

Calculating Interest on Forex Trades

"Treat yourself as your own best friend; with kindness, honesty, and fair play." ~ Fiona Camberun

One of the best things about Forex trading is the fact that one can trade using leverage, thus borrowing as much as 1,000 times your capital in order to make a trade. However, borrowing money for trading in foreign exchange is the same as borrowing it for other purposes—interest must be paid on the loan.

However, as currency trading involves both buying and selling, the interest due on your loan can be offset by the interest earned on the currency you buy. Before going on to particular examples, let us take a look at interest rates in general, to see how the foreign exchange market is affected by it.

In central banks, interest rates are set in accordance with a country's monetary policy—high interest rates make the currency more expensive to buy and lower interest rates make it less so. Imagining the government of a country with high inflation will help you understand how interest rates are used.

The government, because of rapidly rising prices, might decide to raise interest rates. This would increase the cost of the country's currency, and make demand and consumption fall, as borrowing would be more expensive.

This in turn would cause prices to fall and inflation rates would come down. Similarly, a country undergoing recession might lower interest rates to boost the country's economy, as lower price of currency would cause demand, and, therefore, supply, to increase.

Interest rates set by central banks also determine at what rate commercial banks can borrow from governments and lend to their customers, including forex traders. Which tells us how interest rates affect this trade?

A trader who, for example buys GBP/USD, needs to borrow the Dollars to buy the Pounds and will, thus, pay interest on the USD and earn it on the GBP. If the interest rate the Bank of England sets for the UK Pound is higher than the one set by the Federal Reserve for the US Dollar, the trader will earn more on the UK Pounds he bought than he pays on the US Dollars he borrowed, thus making a profit.

However, unless there is a significant difference between the two interest rates, the net profit or loss will be marginal. Besides, while interest rates are set on an annual basis, trading positions are usually opened for short periods. This serves to significantly lower any gain or loss on interest rates.

The Advantages of Automated Forex Trading

"Please think about your legacy, because you are writing it every day." ~ Gary Vaynerchuk

Forex trading is nowadays the preferred form of investment for an increasing number of people these days. It is apparent why this is so.

As the largest trading market in the world, the Forex market has a steadily growing trading volume, which has risen from around $500 billion to about $2 trillion in the last twenty years.

Additionally, since it is not tied to any particular trading floor, it is an unusually liquid market. Operating around the clock also makes it a permanently open market. Thus, since many markets are opening and closing at the same time, one can effectively follow the markets around the world.

Both big and small traders are thus being attracted to Forex trading. They enjoy a wide choice of trading strategies based on the various aspects of the foreign exchange rates. Many traders coming into the market find the different things that affect currency exchange rates very attractive for a very simple reason – they can use a wide range to tools when working in this exciting and stimulating market.

Automation is perhaps the greatest influence today on the future growth of the Forex market, as it brings with it more advantages than disadvantages. Manual systems trying to operate in a fast paced and volatile environment bring with them several losses.

A simple time delay in buying and selling may cause a row of losses in a manual system and thus cause the trader immense frustration. Automated Forex trading allows trade to be conducted anywhere in the world, in real time, and eliminates the losses seen in manual systems.

Operating in a wide range of different currency markets at the same time, without worrying about the time zones of the places concerned, is another advantage that automated Forex trading brings. Sitting in New York at 2 o'clock in the morning, one can conduct business with traders in different countries on the other side of the globe, simultaneously and with great ease. All thanks to automated Forex trading.

Risk management is often a source of worry for traders, but even this is reduced with automated Forex trading. Payments can now be synchronized in real time and this leaves traders satisfied, as opposed to manual trading where there is always uncertainty about payment being made after completion of trade. The automated trading system is developing progressively, and that brings with it hopes that the settlement system will be updated and markets risks will soon cease to exist.

If there is one technology that has advanced by leaps and bounds over the past few years, it is computer technology. Indeed, one hopes that it will continue to grow for many years to come. Most importantly, advances in computer technology spell well for traders who wish to access the best Forex automated trading.

Access to technology easily and cheaply from the comfort of the traders' homes means they can manage their own investments with ease. Automated Forex day trading will thus come as a welcome addition to a fully empowered investment vehicle for those in the currency-trading world.

Choosing the Right Automated Forex Trading Software

"You are the only person that lives with you 24/7/365 so focus on pleasing the person that spends the most time with YOU!" ~ Latoya Garrett

Automated forex trading has a few advantages of its own. Here all you have to do is follow trade signals that are generated and if you are able to execute them with discipline and if your system is logical, then you can easily pile up gains.

Before looking at the various ways you can gain profit through these software, let's take a look at what not to do.

Many traders find forex robots online and buy them. But you must keep in mind that most of these are pieces of junk and have never been traded in real time. Take a look at the track record and then at the disclaimer. It is probably hypothetical or stimulated and that is no sure indication of future results. It is strange how some one can just take a test and claim to make money with it.

Of course, they do make money for the vendor, they get the sale of the software and the trader gets spanked in the market. No one gets 100k annual income for a hundred bucks. You will never make any money with these stimulated systems so try and steer clear of them.

Let's now take a look at how automated forex trading is done in the proper way and discuss the options.

Buy a system with a track record that has been audited over two years. These may not be cheap but they can pay for themselves many times over. You only make sure that you understand and agree with the logic before you begin to use it.

Try the free systems. Look up our other articles to know more about them and you will realize why this is a great place to begin your automated forex trading career.

Go ahead and build your own. This is easier than it sounds. It is also a better way of trading because if you build and customize the system, you will gain more confidence and you will be able to trade with discipline, even during periods of loss.

If you do decide to build yourself a system, we have it covered in our articles. But the best way to go is to trade breakouts, to new highs or lows, have momentum indicators to time your moves and focus on long term trends. The simpler it is the better. This will enable it to face the ever changing market condition. Packing it with too many indicators might break it down.
Once you are in possession of a system, get hold of a forex software package, program the rules and you are all set.

Keep in mind that all forex trading systems, including the best ones will suffer losses that can continue for a long period of time. You need to continue trading until you hit a home run and because of this discipline and money management is necessary.

If your system does between 50-100% compounded annually, you are a part of the best automated forex trading software and you can trade markets and enjoy currency trading success.

FREE BONUS Consulting for Cash Crash Course

Welcome to Consulting for Cash crash course.

The ins and outs of starting your own profitable consulting business.

In this first lesson we are going to talk a little about what is involved in setting up a consulting business and how to know what type of consultant you should be.

Consulting is currently one of the best business models you can follow and it has many rewards including a nice profit margin and plenty of flexibility.

Fact #1: Through consulting, the performance of a business may be substantially improved.

Fact #2: Companies trust the ideas and suggestions of their project team and staff; but most of the time, the expertise need to achieve growth is limited.

Result: This leads to the hiring of private consultants to help the business achieve its goals.

Consulting is a talent. If you have the skills and expertise to help people take their business where they want it to go, then consulting can be a great option with excellent financial returns.

Establishing a consulting business is not always easy, it involves a lot of self-marketing along with a solid reputation and expertise to back it up.

To gain success in consulting, you need to focus on selling one product

- YOU!

But, before you begin marketing yourself you should first determine what your consultant potential is. You can do this by asking yourself a few basic questions.

- What is the thing you are most passionate about?

- What is that thing that you do best?

Once you have determined what that is, ask whether there are people who might need some assistance in that area.

- Now, can you help them?

Of course, you can! You are an expert on it! So why not do it as a business? Earn money helping others with something you know and do best-and that is business consulting.

You can start small. Do it in the comfort of your home as a freelance consultant. There are a lot of organizations and executives out there who are in need of expert consultants and with a little fine tuning, you can become a high-paid advisor.

So what do you need to do next?

Well, as I have said earlier, you have to determine your area of expertise first.

Then find out if you have the required certifications to claim that you are an expert in that field? If you don't, you must secure that first. An expert without credentials is just another person next-door, who is ambitioning to be an expert. People believe in the written word, so you have to have that. However, there are also professions or areas of expertise that doesn't require certificates like fund-raising consultants. Expertise on the likes of this area only needs experience. However, you have to have vast experience in the field you are planning to advise on.

Second, your office, since you are starting small, your first office can be your bedroom, or your study room, if you have one. All you need is a table and chair, an internet connection and a telephone line, and presto! You are almost ready to start your consulting business.

Almost, because you have to understand that though you are starting small, of course, you are also looking to becoming big someday.
So you have to be organized. Consultants are advising on management and that includes time and things management. You have to practice what you are advising.

Third, set your goals and limitations. Why limitations? You are only starting your business, so don't shoot stars. Set your goals to a realizable scale or level. Do not target too many clients and end up failing with your commitments. Be realistic. Do not bite off more than you can chew. Maintain your clientele to a manageable number.

Fourth, develop and make a record of your plan. You need to have a tangible reminder of the path you are taking so you would not go astray. It's easy to get distracted and side-tracked from your goals. So it's best to have it formally written down and give it a professional feel. This way, you can also have something to show possible clients, proving that you are serious in your business.

Fifth, create your lesson plans. Of course, before you can advise, train, or teach, you have to have a lesson plan. You have to know what you are going to tell your clients. Write it on your own. Think of all the possible weakness people might have in your chosen field. Focus and write about that. If you don't know how to start it, begin with the definition of your profession and everything else would follow. The field you are going to write about is your forte, so things should flow easily once you have begun.

As we discussed above, offering consultation services is one of the best business models that you can follow and can provide you with both profits and flexibility.

The typical way to start any type of business is to be as informed as possible about the way it functions. This is also true when running a consulting business.

A good place to start is to purchase informative books, video and other manuals to learn everything you can about the business. You can also seek advice from other consultants who had been successful in their fields. Most of all, don't be shy when it comes to asking for help.

Next, develop a harmonious working relationship with your clients. Building good relationships with the clients is the mantra of all businesses since relationships can go beyond the initial sale and can also forge repeat buys. Clarify client's expectations versus what you can do.

Specify your expertise and the benefits they can get from having you as their consultant. More often than not, clients especially those big organizations have high expectations of the consultants. By being realistic of your capabilities, the good relationship can be developed from then on.

Then, make a good proposal with a clear statement of your strategies and objectives. Since you are the consultant, you are expected to solve majority of the organization's problems. Clearly state on your proposal the services you will provide and the price you will be asking. Strongly emphasize the advantages that your client will enjoy once they deal with you. You can only do this by presenting the benefits they can reap after getting your services.

Now, create a marketing plan to grab the most profitable client's attention. You can briefly present your marketing plan; actually you can devise a seven sentence marketing plan.

- The first sentence explains the purpose of your project.

- Second sentence explains the ways on how to achieve the purpose and the benefits that the clients can get.

- Third sentence describes the target market.

- Fourth sentence describes the niche.

- Fifth sentence is about the weapons you will utilize.

- Sixth sentence is about your business identity.

- And the seventh is all about the budget.

Present a refined, professional image. Being in the image business, your clients will perceive you as an ultimate maker of sales. One sure way to draw new clients is to be categorized as an expert in the consulting industry.

Project yourself as an expert having marketable skills produced from a combination of education and knowledge you gained from years of experience. Since your skills are rare, many companies will be willing to pay your premium. But they also need to see you as in demand, successful and one of the top quality consultants of all time. Make sure that you have all the necessary materials such as sample videos and business cards. Convey an image of an expert who have all the knowledge clients can benefit from.

Consider offering a free introductory session when needed. Often, consultants are conscious of the bills and are hesitant to give their services. Being a consultant does not always mean charging per hour of your precious service. If you are just starting with your business, you must first build client's awareness about your services so free short consultation will not hurt you. Ensure that your client will be interested on your services by conducting free information seminar once in a while. This can give you exposure and referrals.

Be keen with results. The clearest path to have new clients is a promotion from those who saw your first successful project. Keep your network of employers and other persons that you know. Always keep in mind that in consulting business, results are the viable tool to acquire clients. To be successful, you must deliver and offer undisputed value to your clients and all other members of your network.

These are just some simple steps that can be followed when starting a new consulting business. This might not be enough though since a great effort must be exerted when running any chosen business. With all these ingredients, your consulting business will surely give you huge money.

I know, I know... You must be thinking that I'm crazy, suggesting that you offer your business consulting for free. We touched briefly on this earlier and as we move forward I feel it is important that you understand the benefits of offering your services for free.

The big question you may be asking yourself is; "How can I make money by providing my consulting services for free?" You may be thinking that will turn your business into a charity, right?

Wrong!

What I'm talking about here is giving out free consultancy as a teaser, a free taste or free sample, so to speak. People don't just buy new products from a stranger without testing the product first. When you are just getting started chances are that you aren't very well-known, so it will be more difficult to get new clients to invest in you.

Nobody invests in something that is not reliable to generate good results. Unless you are backed by someone very famous and reliable, you are not going to get clients for your business.

By providing free consultancies, you are giving them a taste of what it is like to have you as a consultant. You are not going to hand them everything you have got in a silver platter. No, that's not what I am saying. It just about giving them a free sample-a small sachet of your service. It is a very good way of enticing and luring them to your business. Once you have proven that you can help them and you made them happy with the result of your sample service, they are left with little choice but to hire your services. They wouldn't be able to deny a good tangible result!

So, what you have to do is advertise on your social media, blog, website that you are offering free business consulting. Nothing lures customer more effectively than the screaming word "FREE". People's weaknesses always include freebies.

Create a downloadable request for consulting form on your website so that they can send you their contact information and initial details of their consulting needs. This would also give you chance to build your list of possible clients as they would be leaving their company's contact information and their own contact information as well.

Once you have gained enough names on your list, try to become friends with them. In every business, good relationship is the key. So don't just build mountains of contacts, but build networks of relationships.

Establish a good working relationship with everyone you meet in your free consulting services, and you are sure to get referrals. This way, you are slowly building a network that would work for you and your business.

When you have lots of friends in the business world who believe in your talent, they would surely tap you in every endeavor related to your expertise.

Soon afterwards, you would find yourself speaking at their conferences or seminars like what I do. And that is another opportunity for you to market yourself and your business consulting services. You can do the public speeches for free, too! This way, you are establishing goodwill and gaining their trust. And in a way, they become indebted to you and would doubtlessly return the favor in the future.

Offering free business consulting services and free public speeches are even better and cheaper than advertisements using professional advertising agencies. You can also consider it as a practice in honing your consulting skills. But of course, you still do your own advertising from your own website, publishing newsletters and distributing brochures and leaflets.

It boiled down to this; now we are going to jump right into some of the things that you should know about running a consulting business. Remember, you don't have to reinvent the wheel. You just have to have the right mind set and the proper information to get on the right track.

According to the Harvard Business School research, about 100 billion dollars are generated by the business consulting industry. This is from the annual revenues gained by consultants solely in the United States. Consultants are really needed by companies in a slow economy to assist them in cutting their costs and increasing their revenues.

As a business consultant, you will be relied on and respected in every industry and in every country. Being a business consultant, you will be admired for both your independence and expertise.

The bottom line of business consulting is to help organization leverage their business performances to produce viable results. Among the services that can be offered by business consulting are:

- Improving productivity.

You can assist your clients to work more efficiently or redesign the work processes. You can also institutionalize and design metrics for process enhancements.

- Optimizing workload and applications.

You can help clients align applications for business strategy, plan internal resources and prioritize critical work requests.

- Ensuring effective outsourcing.

You can also ensure the outsourcing suitability of the organizations infrastructure and applications. You can also help them design governance structure that will lead to better management of relationship issues and organizational change.

You can also choose to specialize in other different areas such as:

Marketing consulting,
Small business consulting,
Communications consulting,
Organizational development consulting,
Coaching Consulting
IT consulting,
Strategic planning consulting,
HR consulting and any other areas that need professional advice.

With all the expertise gained by a business consultant, it's no wonder that they are one of the most highly paid professionals. On a recent survey conducted by Association of Management Consulting Firms, it was found out that entry level consultants earn an average annual income of $65,000 or more.

When it comes to being a highly sought after consultant just remember that hard work and perseverance equates the profit and fame that you may acquire from this business. There are also some good rules of thumb that you should always keep in mind:

You and the client should have a good working relationship. Establish a relationship that will go beyond your first sale. Clarify the expectations from your first assignment. Describe the things that you do and identify the benefits a client will achieve. Clients hire you because of your skills and expertise so you should be able to produce a quality work for them.

You are hired as a consultant to help the client's problem; clearly state your proposal that is beneficial enough for the client, that way the price that you are asking them is worth the pay. From your proposal, let them feel that they really need your expertise. Always emphasize the benefits that they will obtain from your services.

Always present a professional image. The client's perception of what you are really important. Always show them that you have the expertise and skills that are highly based on the combination of your education and knowledge from your chosen field. Because of this, client would willingly pay you because your skills will help them improve their firms. Always keep in mind that clients expect to see an in demand and successful business consultant.

You are just establishing a consulting business, so offer free sessions. This will be the chance for you to expose yourself and gain referrals. Always keep in mind that as a starting consultant you need not bill them right away. First, think of ways you can help them, not monetize every hour you talk to them.

Charge your clients by your hourly rate, not by the whole job. A consultant is being paid for the hours that will be used for the project. Make sure that the rate your rate is equivalent to your expertise, type of field and your contracting firm's size. Also, include in your fees the overhead expenses, the time spent in marketing and other administrative endeavors.

Make an update of your client's portfolio. It's not bad to remove clients that generate small income. After all, you are talking about your own business here. You can get referrals from good clients and even fish for some new industries to widen your horizon. But remember; take on the assignments that you think you will enjoy and never forget to follow up for your clients.

These are just a few simple guidelines that will help you establish a successful consulting business. Entering the business consulting arena can be a daunting task, but if you have the needed skills and expertise, you'll have no problem becoming successful in this field.

Just remember that, business consulting is a win-win situation if you are a good consultant. You can help improve other firms and also improve your consulting business. So start your consulting business and move your way for a higher income.

Here I will be dishing out some great ways to help keep your consulting business sustainable and profitable for years to come.

Like every other business endeavor, business consulting has its own risks. There will always be doubts and second thoughts and lots and lots of after thoughts. Nothing in this life is sure to last forever.

In fact, nothing really will last forever. So if what you want is to have a business that would last forever, you are trying to hit the moon. However, there is always hope, to keep your business afloat and thriving in the jungle world of entrepreneurship for a very long time.

Yes, there is always hope. But you have to work really hard for that hope to materialize. The best thing you can aim at is keeping your business consulting firm sustainable. If you can achieve that, then you can start working on keeping it abreast with other companies in the field.

So how do you keep your consulting business sustainable? You only have a few contacts or connections, so what happens when you have used up your existing resources?

Simple. Create and build new resources. The only way to keep your business going is to have an ample supply of resources. So, here are a few things you could do to keep business going and growing.

First thing to do is to firmly establish your business plan. You are going to engage in a very serious business so you have to be serious about.

Your clients should take you as a serious, no-nonsense person that would deliver them good results. So do your homework and be prepared.

Have a comprehensive business kit containing details of your services in a neatly packaged brochure, with hourly rates, project rates, retainer basis rate and whatever package you want to serve your client.

This brochure would be your salesperson in your absence, so make it the best brochure you can ever make. This is the blood of your business, keeps it pulsing through your veins.

Second is finding clients. You can find clients through friends' referrals but that would not last very long. Even if you have a long list of friends, that is still not enough to last your business a lifetime.

So you have to exert more effort. Try cold calling. It may sound a little to below your level, but hey, this is business! You need to do whatever it takes to get clients and cold calling is not as bad as you may think. You just have to do it right and do it nicely.

You know how irritating it is to be offered things over the phone, so try not to be irritating. Try not to do the things that those telemarketers do to irritate you.

Prepare a nice introductory script before making your first call. Try not to bombard your prospective client with the details of your business. Your goal is to get him interested enough to agree on a meeting with you for further discussion of your services.

It also pays to remember that very person you meet, great or small is a possible connection. So be nice to all people all the time. He may just be a janitor or a food attendant at a restaurant, but for all you know, you may be talking the person who could lead you to your biggest catch ever. So be nice all the time.

As we close this final lesson I would like to thank you again for joining me and I sincerely hope that you have learned a lot about how to start your own profitable consulting business!

No! Clients No! Lists! Don't stress you are all covered.

Please feel free to contact me if you have any questions. I will be glad to help!

You're Ready, Now get prepared for Special Self development Ultimate proven formula for success™

"Life with Woody" 10 inspirational quotes than can improve yourself

It might take a little coffee or probably a few rounds of beer or any other booze you could get your hands on when it comes to relaxing after a hard day's work. Well, yeah I'm guilty about that one as well, unless I'm caught dead wearing a lampshade over my head after a few rounds of vodka... half-naked! Okay, bad example and I apologize to everyone reading this after getting nightmares about me in that state of drunken stupor.

Just don't ask how it happened, please.

But what's really interesting is that how do people go through the usual part of life when faced with vein-popping stress? I mean, the new age thing like Zen or yoga is one of the good things and it actually works. Is there room for the intellectual side of people who can actually smell the roses-in-a-can while on the move? It kind of had me thinking that there really must be something in this 'mind-over-matter' thing.

Humor is indeed the best medicine there is whenever you are. I mean anyone can pay good money to listen to a comedian just to make you wet your pants after laughing so hard. Despite of what's been happening, and to those who has gone though the ordeal, it's better to just laugh while facing the troubles with a clear mind than anger with a clouded vision. One of my favorite celebrities of all time may have to be Woody Allen. Now this is one guy who gives you the in-your-face bluntness that he pulls out with gusto, even without even trying. You can talk just about anything with a man, and he's bound to mock the subject and you'll end up laughing rather than being upset about it.

Woody Allen has this to say:

1. "Money is better than poverty, if only for financial reasons." It sounds good to me, I mean the practicality of all things does involve money but it doesn't have to take an arm and a leg to get it.

2. "I believe there is something out there watching us. Unfortunately, it's the government." 'Nuff said.

3. "There are worse things in life than death. Have you ever spent an evening with an insurance salesman?" This happens to be one of the classic ones. I mean the issue about life's little problems isn't all that bad, until 'he' shows up.

Sure, relationships can get complicated, or does have its complications that probably any author about relationships is bound to discover it soon. We follow what our heart desires, unless you're talking about the heart as in the heart that pumps blood throughout your body.

4. "Love is the answer, but while you're waiting for the answer, sex raises some pretty interesting questions." And if you want more, just keep on asking!

5. "A fast word about oral contraception. I asked a girl to go to bed with me, she said 'no'." It sounds, 'practical', I think.

And when it comes to everyday life, he really knows how to make the best out of every possible scenario, and it doesn't involve a lawsuit if he strikes a nerve.

6. "Basically my wife was immature. I'd be at home in the bath and she'd come in and sink my boats." I never had a boat in my bathtub before. Just staring at it while soaking in hot water makes me seasick already.

7. "I am not afraid of death; I just don't want to be there when it happens." If it rains, it pours.

8. "I am thankful for laughter, except when milk comes out of my nose." It could get worse when you're guzzling on beer... or mouthwash and it happened to me once!

9. "If you want to make God laugh, tell him about your plans." At least he doesn't smite us with lightning, and I'm thankful for that.

And despite of what may happen to all of us in the next ten, twenty, or even thirty years, I guess we all have to see things in a different kind of light and not just perspective. I can't seem to imagine life without any piece of wisdom that could guide us. Whether we're religious or not, it takes more courage to accept your fears and learn how to deal with them is all that matters when it comes to even just getting along.

And to sum things up, here is the last nugget of wisdom to go by... however, whenever, and wherever we may be.

10. "The talent for being happy is appreciating and liking what you have, instead of what you don't have."

"What Really Makes You Tick?" 10 questions you should ask to yourself: a preparation to self-improvement

Be all you can be, but it's not always in the Army. I often see myself as somewhat contented with my life the way things are, but of course it's hard to think of anything else when where are real issues to be discussed.

Still I aspire for something deeper and more meaningful.

So we're all pelted with problems. Honestly it shouldn't even bother or even hinder us to becoming all we ought to be. Aspirations as kids should continue to live within us, even though it would be short-lived or as long as we could hold on to the dream. They say you can't teach an old dog new tricks... or can they?

1. What do I really want?
The question of the ages. So many things you want to do with your life and so little time to even go about during the day.

Find something that you are good at can help realize that small step towards improvement. Diligence is the key to know that it is worth it.

2. Should I really change?
Today's generation has taken another level of redefining 'self', or at least that's what the kids are saying. Having an army of teenage nieces and nephews has taught me that there are far worse things that they could have had than acne or maybe even promiscuity. So how does that fit into your lifestyle?

If history has taught us one thing, it's the life that we have gone through. Try to see if partying Seventies style wouldn't appeal to the younger generation, but dancing is part of partying. Watch them applaud after showing them how to really dance than break their bones in break-dancing.

3. What's the bright side in all of this?
With so much is happening around us there seem to be no room for even considering that light at the end of the tunnel. We can still see it as something positive without undergoing so much scrutiny. And if it's a train at the end of the tunnel, take it for a ride and see what makes the world go round!

4. Am I comfortable with what I'm doing?
There's always the easy way and the right way when it comes to deciding what goes with which shoes, or purse, shirt and whatnot. It doesn't take a genius to see yourself as

someone unique, or else we'll all be equally the same in everything we do. Variety brings in very interesting and exciting questions to be experimented.

5. Have I done enough for myself?
Have you, or is there something more you want to do? Discontentment in every aspect can be dangerous in large doses, but in small amounts you'll be able to see and do stuff you could never imagine doing.

6. Am I happy at where I am today?
It's an unfair question so let it be an answer! You love being a good and loving mom or dad to your kids, then take it up a notch! Your kids will love you forever. The same goes with everyday life!

7. Am I appealing to the opposite sex?
So maybe I don't have an answer to that, but that doesn't mean I can't try it, though. Whether you shape-up, change the way you wear your clothes or hair, or even your attitude towards people, you should always remember it will always be for your own benefit.

8. How much could I have?
I suppose in this case there is no such things on having things too much or too little, but it's more on how badly you really need it. I'd like to have lots of money, no denying that, but the question is that how much are you willing to work for it?

9. What motivates me?
What motivates you? It's an answer you have to find out for yourself. There are so many things that can make everyone happy, but to choose one of the may be the hardest part. It's not like you can't have one serving of your favorite food in a buffet and that's it. Just try it piece by piece.

10. What Really Makes You Tick?
So? What really makes you tick? You can be just about anything you always wanted to be, but to realize that attaining something that may seem very difficult is already giving up before you even start that journey.

"A Piece of Blarney Stone" 10 ways to empower your communication

The Blarney Stone is a historical stone, or actually part of the Blarney Castle in Ireland where it was believed that kissing the stone can grant you the gift of gab. Yeah, it seems strange in this day and age, but who are we to question tradition? It's not like I'm saying that Santa Claus doesn't exist (OOPS!).

There is so much to know about conversation that anyone, even I, could ever realize. You can go though watching talk shows; radio programs; clubs dedicated to public speaking; ordinary conversations; certain rules still apply when it comes to interaction through words. It may sound tedious, I know, but even though it's your mouth that's doing the work, your brain works twice as hard to churn out a lot of things you know. So what better way to start learning to be an effective communication is to know the very person closest to you: yourself.

1. What you know.
Education is all about learning the basics, but to be an effective speaker is to practice what you've learned. My stint as guest at every Toastmasters' meeting I go to taught me that we all have our limitations, but that doesn't mean we can't learn to keep up and share what we know.

2. Listening.
It's just as important as asking questions. Sometimes listening to the sound of our own voice can teach us to be a little bit confident with ourselves and to say the things we believe in with conviction.

3. Humility
We all make mistakes, and sometimes we tend to slur our words, stutter, and probably mispronounce certain words even though we know what it means, but rarely use it only to impress listeners. So in a group, don't be afraid to ask if you're saying the right word properly and if they're unsure about it then make a joke out of it. I promise you it'll make everyone laugh and you can get away with it as well.

4. Eye Contact
There's a lot to say when it comes to directing your attention to your audience with an eye-catching gaze. It's important that you keep your focus when talking to a large group in a meeting or a gathering, even though he or she may be gorgeous.

5. Kidding around
A little bit of humor can do wonders to lift the tension, or worse boredom when making your speech. That way, you'll get the attention of the majority of the crowd and they'll feel that you're just as approachable, and as human to those who listen.

6. Be like the rest of them

Interaction is all about mingling with other people. You'll get a lot of ideas, as well as knowing what people make them as they are.

7. Me, Myself, and I

Admit it, there are times you sing to yourself in the shower. I know I do! Listening to the sound of your own voice while you practice your speech in front of a mirror can help correct the stress areas of your pitch. And while you're at it you can spruce up as well.

8. with a smile

A smile says it all much like eye contact. There's no point on grimacing or frowning in a meeting or a gathering, unless it's a wake. You can better express what you're saying when you smile.

9. A Role Model

There must be at least one or two people in your life you have listened to when they're at a public gathering or maybe at church. Sure they read their lines, but taking a mental note of how they emphasize what they say can help you once you take center stage.

10. Preparation

Make the best out of preparation rather than just scribbling notes and often in a hurried panic. Some people like to write things down on index cards, while other resort to being a little more silly as they look at their notes written on the palm of their hand (not for clammy hands, please). Just be comfortable with what you know since you enjoy your work.

And that about wraps it up. These suggestions are rather amateurish in edgewise, but I've learned to empower myself when it comes to public or private speaking and it never hurts to be with people to listen how they make conversations and meetings far more enjoyable as well as education

"Who's the Boss?" 10 ways to start taking control (time management, goal setting, and record tracking)

At first glance, it would seem that positive thinking and Attention Deficit Disorder (ADD) have nothing to do with one another. But many of us with ADD develop negative thinking patterns because we become frustrated by our challenges and frequent feelings of being overwhelmed. This negative outlook then makes it even harder for us to manage those challenges and move forward.

Practicing positive thinking allows people with ADD to focus on our strengths and accomplishments, which increases happiness and motivation. This, in turn, allows us to spend more time making progress, and less time feeling down and stuck. The following tips provide practical suggestions that you can use to help you shift into more positive thinking patterns:

1. Take Good Care of Yourself
It's much easier to be positive when you are eating well, exercising, and getting enough rest.

2. Remind Yourself of the Things You Are Grateful For
Stresses and challenges don't seem quite as bad when you are constantly reminding yourself of the things that are right in life. Taking just 60 seconds a day to stop and appreciate the good things will make a huge difference.

3. Look for the Proof Instead of Making Assumptions
A fear of not being liked or accepted sometimes leads us to assume that we know what others are thinking, but our fears are usually not reality. If you have a fear that a friend or family member's bad mood is due to something you did, or that your co-workers are secretly gossiping about you when you turn your back, speak up and ask them. Don't waste time worrying that you did something wrong unless you have proof that there is something to worry about.

4. Refrain from Using Absolutes
Have you ever told a partner "You're ALWAYS late!" or complained to a friend "You NEVER call me!"? Thinking and speaking in absolutes like 'always' and 'never' makes the situation seem worse than it is, and programs your brain into believing that certain people are incapable of delivering.

5. Detach From Negative Thoughts
Your thoughts can't hold any power over you if you don't judge them. If you notice yourself having a negative thought, detach from it, witness it, and don't follow it.

6. Squash the "ANTs"
In his book "Change Your Brain, Change Your Life," Dr. Daniel Amen talks about "ANTs" - Automatic Negative Thoughts. These are the bad thoughts that are usually reactionary, like "Those people are laughing, they must be talking about me," or "The boss wants to see me? It must be bad!" When you notice these thoughts, realize that they are nothing more than ANTs and squash them!

7. Practice Lovin', Touchin' & Squeezin' (Your Friends and Family)
You don't have to be an expert to know the benefits of a good hug. Positive physical contact with friends, loved ones, and even pets, is an instant pick-me-up. One research study on this subject had a waitress touch some of her customers on the arm as she handed them their checks. She received higher tips from these customers than from the ones she didn't touch!

8. Increase Your Social Activity
By increasing social activity, you decrease loneliness. Surround yourself with healthy, happy people, and their positive energy will affect you in a positive way!

9. Volunteer for an Organization, or Help another Person
Everyone feels good after helping. You can volunteer your time, your money, or your resources. The more positive energy you put out into the world, the more you will receive in return.

10. Use Pattern Interrupts to Combat Rumination
If you find yourself ruminating, a great way to stop it is to interrupt the pattern and force yourself to do something completely different. Rumination is like hyper-focus on something negative. It's never productive, because it's not rational or solution-oriented, it's just excessive worry. Try changing your physical environment - go for a walk or sit outside. You could also call a friend, pick up a book, or turn on some music.

When it comes to the corporate world, protocol is pretty much the religion. To know the things needed to do are the basics of productivity, but interaction and having a steady mind makes up the entire thing to true productivity. There are those who seem to work well even under pressure, but they're uncommon ones and we are human and imperfect. To get these little things like stress under our skins won't solve our problems. Sometimes it takes a bit of courage to admit that we're turning to be workaholics than tell ourselves that we're not doing our best.

Happy as You Want to Be

Almost everyone have heard the hit single 'Don't Worry, Be Happy' by Bobby McFerrin. The song has a very catchy way of conveying its message of being happy to everyone.

Bobby Mcferiin's simple message surely made a lot of people by telling them not to worry.

Living a happy, resilient and optimistic life is wonderful, and is also good for your health. Being happy actually protects you from the stresses of life. Stress is linked to top causes of death such as heart disease, cancer and stroke.

One of the better things ever said is - 'The only thing in life that will always remain the same is change', and in our life we have the power to make the necessary changes if we want to. Even if we find ourselves in an unbearable situation we can always find solace in the knowledge that it too would change.

Social networks or relationships are essential to happiness. People are different, accept people for who or what they are, avoid clashes, constant arguments, and let go of all kinds of resentments. If arguments seem unavoidable still try and make an effort to understand the situation and you might just get along with well with

Happiness is actually found in everyone, increasing it is a way to make a life more wonderful and also healthier.

To be happy is relatively easy; just decide to be a happy person. Abraham Lincoln observed that most people for most of the time can choose how happy or stressed, how relaxed or troubled, how bright or dull their outlook to be. The choice is simple really, choose to be happy.

There are several ways by which you can do this.

Being grateful is a great attitude. We have so much to be thankful for. Thank the taxi driver for bringing you home safely, thank the cook for a wonderful dinner and thank the guy who cleans your windows. Also thank the mailman for bringing you your mails, thank the policeman for making your place safe and thank God for being alive.

News is stressful. Get less of it. Some people just can't start their day without their daily dose of news. Try and think about it, 99% of the news we hear or read is bad news. Starting the day with bad news does not seem to be a sensible thing to do.

A religious connection is also recommended. Being part of a religious group with its singing, sacraments, chanting, prayers and meditations foster inner peace.

Manage your time. Time is invaluable and too important to waste. Time management can be viewed as a list of rules that involves scheduling, setting goals, planning, creating lists of things to do and prioritizing. These are the core basics of time management that should be understood to develop an efficient personal time management skill. These basic skills can be fine tuned further to include the finer points of each skill that can give you that extra reserve to make the results you desire.

Laugh and laugh heartily everyday. Heard a good joke? Tell your friends or family about it. As they also say -'Laughter is the best medicine'.

Express your feelings, affections, friendship and passion to people around you. They will most likely reciprocate your actions. Try not to keep pent up anger of frustrations, this is bad for your health. Instead find ways of expressing them in a way that will not cause more injury or hurt to anyone.

Working hard brings tremendous personal satisfaction. It gives a feeling of being competent in finishing our tasks. Accomplishments are necessary for all of us; they give us a sense of value. Work on things that you feel worthy of your time.

Learning is a joyful exercise. Try and learn something new everyday. Learning also makes us expand and broaden our horizons. And could also give us more opportunities in the future.

Run, jog, walk and do other things that your body was made for. Feel alive.

Avoid exposure to negative elements like loud noises, toxins and hazardous places.

These are the few simple things you can do everyday to be happy.

And always remember the quote from Abraham Lincoln; he says that, "Most people are about as happy as they make up their minds to be."

What Innovation Can Do to Your Life

It's a talent that everyone has, yet they think they don't. The power of innovation. If you've ever marvelled at somebody's creative prowess, guess what, you can create and innovate too. It just takes time. Everyone is born creative. The box of crayons in kindergarten were not limited to those who possessed potential; because the truth is, everybody has potential.

You know how long it took to learn to ride a bike or drive or to never commit the same mistake again? It's the same with innovation. It takes a bit of practice and a lot of time before this mind function comes easily when called. This article will teach you a few tips on how to bring innovation into your life.

Don't listen to what other people say. Follow the beat of your own drum. Allowing for the input of other people will only bring cacophony to the music you are trying to make. If you have an original idea, don't waste your time and effort trying to make people understand. They won't. And the help you will probably get comes in the form of negative feedback. If all those geniuses listened to their peers, we would probably still be living in the middle ages.

Spend time on it. I cannot stress that enough, although, please do not mistake this tip to tell you to quit your day job entirely. Do not. This involves some tricky time management but with a little discipline you'll be able to squeeze both in.

Exercise. Take a walk. Run a mile or two. Send all those endorphins coursing through your veins. Exercising certainly clears and relaxes your mind and allows for anything to pop up.

Record your dreams. Aren't some of them just the craziest things that your conscious mind would never have thought of? If you've had these dreams before, and I'm sure have, this only shows you the untapped innovative power you have lying within. So jot down those notes. Those dreams may just create an innovative spark in you.

Find your own style. You can always tell a Van Gogh from a Matisse. You'll know Hemingway wrote something by the choice of words on the paper. So it is the same with you. People will appreciate your innovation more because it is uniquely yours and that no one else would have thought of what you were thinking. That will let people see how valuable an asset you are.

Don't hide behind nifty gadgets or tools. You don't need the most expensive set of paints to produce a masterpiece. The same way with writing. You don't need some expensive fountain pen and really smooth paper for a bestseller. In fact, J.K. Rowling wrote the first book of the Harry Potter Series on bits of tissue. So what if you've got an expensive SLR camera if you're a crappy photographer? Who cares if you've got a blinging laptop if you can't write at all? The artist actually reduces the number of tools he has as he gets better at his craft: he knows what works and what doesn't.

Nothing will work without passion. What wakes you up in the mornings? What keeps the flame burning? What is the one thing that you'll die if you don't do? Sometimes people with talent are overtaken by the people who want it more. Think the hare and the tortoise. Ellen Degeneres once said that if you're not doing something that you want to do, then you don't really want to do it. And that's true. Sometimes you just want something so bad you become a virtual unstoppable. And that is passion. Passion will keep you going.

Don't worry about inspiration. You can't force it; inspiration hits when you least expect it to, for those unpredictable yet inevitable moments you should prepare. An idea could strike you on the subway, yet alas, you poor unfortunate soul; you have no sheet of paper to scribble down a thought that could change the world. Avoid these disasters. Have a pen and paper within your arm's reach at all times.

I hope this article has helped you bring more innovation into your life. Keep in mind that you're doing these things for your own satisfaction and not anybody else's. But soon enough they will notice and everything should snowball from there.

Build your self esteem, a starter guide to self improvement

So how do you stay calm, composed and maintain self esteem in a tough environment? Here are some tips you may to consider as a starter guide to self improvement.

Imagine yourself as a Dart Board. Everything and everyone else around you may become Dart Pins, at one point or another. These dart pins will destroy your self esteem and pull you down in ways you won't even remember. Don't let them destroy you, or get the best of you. So which dart pins should you avoid?

Dart Pin #1 : Negative Work Environment
Beware of "dog eat dog" theory where everyone else is fighting just to get ahead. This is where non-appreciative people usually thrive. No one will appreciate your contributions even if you miss lunch and dinner, and stay up late. Most of the time you get to work too much without getting help from people concerned. Stay out of this; it will ruin your self esteem. Competition is at stake anywhere. Be healthy enough to compete, but in a healthy competition that is.

Dart Pin #2: Other People's Behavior
Bulldozers, brown nosers, gossipmongers, whiners, backstabbers, snipers, people walking wounded, controllers, naggers, complainers, exploders, patronizers, sluffers… all these kinds of people will pose bad vibes for your self esteem, as well as to your self improvement scheme.

Dart Pin #3: Changing Environment
You can't be a green bug on a brown field. Changes challenge our paradigms. It tests our flexibility, adaptability and alters the way we think. Changes will make life difficult for awhile, it may cause stress but it will help us find ways to improve our selves. Change will be there forever, we must be susceptible to it.

Dart Pin #4: Past Experience
It's okay to cry and say "ouch!" when we experience pain. But don't let pain transform itself into fear. It might grab you by the tail and swing you around. Treat each failure and mistake as a lesson.

Dart Pin #5: Negative World View
Look at what you're looking at. Don't wrap yourself up with all the negativities of the world. In building self esteem, we must learn how to make the best out of worst situations.

Dart Pin #6: Determination Theory
The way you are and your behavioral traits is said to be a mixed end product of your inherited traits (genetics), your upbringing (psychic), and your environmental surroundings such as your spouse, the company, the economy or your circle of friends.

You have your own identity. If your father is a failure, it doesn't mean you have to be a failure too. Learn from other people's experience, so you'll never have to encounter the same mistakes.

Sometimes, you may want to wonder if some people are born leaders or positive thinkers. NO. Being positive, and staying positive is a choice. Building self esteem and drawing lines for self improvement is a choice, not a rule or a talent. God wouldn't come down from heaven and tell you – "George, you may now have the permission to build self esteem and improve your self."

In life, its hard to stay tough specially when things and people around you keep pulling you down. When we get to the battle field, we should choose the right luggage to bring and armors to use, and pick those that are bullet proof. Life's options give us arrays of more options. Along the battle, we will get hit and bruised. And wearing bullet proof armor ideally means 'self change'. The kind of change which comes from within. Voluntarily. Armor or Self Change changes 3 things: our attitude, our behavior and our way of thinking.

Building self esteem will eventually lead to self improvement if we start to become responsible for who we are, what we have and what we do. It's like a flame that should gradually spread like a brush fire from inside and out. When we develop self esteem, we take control of our mission, values and discipline. Self esteem brings about self improvement, true assessment, and determination. So how do you start putting up the building blocks of self esteem? Be positive. Be contented and happy. Be appreciative. Never miss an opportunity to compliment. A positive way of living will help you build self esteem, your starter guide to self improvement.

The Road to Intuition

Have you had that experience when all of a sudden you just had this huge hunch that something is about to happen, and to your surprise, that intuition was eventually translated to reality?

When you feel strongly about something without logical basis to it, that's called intuition. It comes in three impressions: clairvoyance or "the third eye", sensing clearly and feeling through listening.

Clairvoyance is when your eye goes beyond what it can see. This is when you know what is happening somewhere.

Sensing clearly is basically what we refer to as "hunch" or "gut feel." This is the time when you are overwhelmed with a feeling and you can't explain it and all you can say is "I just know."

On the other hand, feeling through listening or clairaudience is being able to "listen" between the lines. Intuition also happens at times when a certain sound, whatever it is - be it a car's honk or a bird's twitting - ushers in an intense feeling.

They say only a number of people are gifted with intuition. Astrologers even insist that people born under the Scorpio or Pisces signs are naturally intuitive it almost borders on E.S.P. But studies have been sprouting left and right that proclaim that anyone can develop intuition.

Why the need to develop intuition, you ask? Why not let your emotional and psychological state as it is? First and foremost, intuition promotes good communication. It makes you more sensitive to the people around you; it often keeps you from hurting those you love because you are intuitive enough to understand them. Intuition also makes you far more creative than ever. Intuition means releasing more creative juices for any means of expression. Lastly, intuition has a healing power. This healing power is not in the physical sense, but in delving deep into your soul to eradicate some negative energy buried in it.

With that being said, are you ready to develop your intuition? Here are some ways to unlock this gift:

1. Hypnosis

Oh yes, get yourself hypnotized. Hypnosis is not limited to watching a pendulum move back and forth. Perform self-hypnosis or you can avail of hypnotic programs that can strengthen your intuition.

2. Meditation

Meditating means finding peace in yourself. If your mind and heart are cluttered with too many baggage and hurt, you wouldn't be able to quiet down that part of you that could eventually initiate intuition. There are so many ways to meditate: take a yoga class, or just simply practice some breathing that could bring you straight to Zen.

3. Think positive!

A worry-free, fear-free state could do so much to improve your intuitive ability. By staying positive, you attract good energy that would be able to easily recognize imminent feelings and events.

4. Just let go.

What does this mean? If you are on the brink of making a huge decision, let go of all the inhibitions and head to a quiet place where you could find out where the letting go has brought you. Sometimes you just have to listen to the voice within you, and that voice wouldn't come out unless you let go.

5. Never expect.

After letting go of the inhibitions and all those things that stop you from thinking and feeling clearly, never expect for an answer right away. Never expect that the "hunch" would fall on your lap immediately. Give it a little time then you'd just get surprised that -- wham! -- now you have your answer.

6. Believe in your first impressions.

When you see someone for the first time and think that he is a bit too arrogant for your taste, chances are that impression actually holds true. Most of the time, first impressions are brought by intuition.

7. Stay happy!

See? All you need to be intuitive is to stay happy! Happiness attracts immense power and such power includes intuition. In tapping your intuition, your motivation must be happiness and contentment. Given that premise, intuition will fall to you easily.

Intuition is helpful, because sometimes it leads you to something that cannot be achieved otherwise. A lot of lives have been saved by intuition alone. Decisions are easier done if armed by this gift. Develop intuition now and reap benefits you have never imagined.

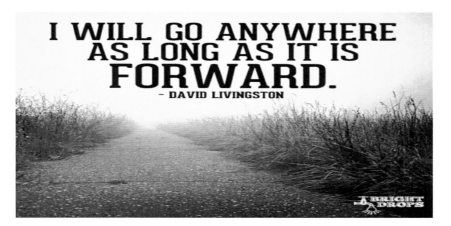

Impossible is Just a Word

Everyone, at some point of his or her life, has dreamed of being somebody special, somebody big. Who hasn't fantasized about being the one who hits the game-winning homer? Who hasn't dreamed of being the homecoming queen? And how many times have we dreamed of being rich, or successful, or happy with our relationships?

Often, we dream big dreams and have great aspirations. Unfortunately, our dreams remain just that – dreams. And our aspirations easily collect dust in our attic.

This is a sad turn of events in our life. Instead of experiencing exciting adventures in self actualization, we get caught up in the humdrum of living from day-to-day just barely existing.

But you know what? Life could be so much better, if only we learned to aim higher.

The most common problem to setting goals is the word impossible. Most people get hung up thinking I can't do this. It's too hard. It's too impossible. No one can do this.

However, if everyone thought that, there would be no inventions, no innovations, and no breakthroughs in human accomplishment.

Remember that scientists were baffled when they took a look at the humble bumblebee. Theoretically, they said, it was impossible for the bumblebee to fly. Unfortunately for the bumble, bee no one has told it so. So fly it does.

On the other hand, some people suffer from dreaming totally outrageous dreams and not acting on them. The result? Broken dreams, and tattered aspirations.

If you limit yourself with self-doubt, and self-limiting assumptions, you will never be able to break past what you deem impossible. If you reach too far out into the sky without working towards your goal, you will find yourself clinging on to the impossible dream.

Try this exercise. Take a piece of paper and write down some goals in your life. Under one header, list down things 'you know you can do'. Under another header, write the things 'you might be able to do.' And under one more, list the things that that are 'impossible for you to do.'

Now look at all the headers strive every day to accomplish the goals that are under things 'you know you can do'. Check them when you are able to accomplish them. As you slowly are able to check all of your goals under that heading, try accomplishing the goals under the other header-the one that reads 'you might be able to do.'

As of the items you wrote under things I could do are accomplished, you can move the goals that are under things that are 'impossible for you to do' to the list of things 'you might be able to do.'

As you iterate through this process, you will find out that the goals you thought were impossible become easier to accomplish. And the impossible begin to seem possible after all.

You see, the technique here is not to limit your imagination. It is to aim high, and start working towards that goal little by little. However, it also is unwise to set a goal that is truly unrealistic.

Those who just dream towards a goal without working hard end up disappointed and disillusioned.

On the other hand, if you told someone a hundred years ago that it was possible for man to be on the moon, they would laugh at you. If you had told them that you could send mail from here to the other side of the world in a few seconds, they would say you were out of your mind. But, through sheer desire and perseverance, these impossible dreams are now realities.

Thomas Edison once said that genius is 1% inspiration and 99% perspiration. Nothing could be truer. For one to accomplish his or her dreams, there has to be had work and discipline. But take note that that 1% has to be a think-big dream, and not some easily accomplished one.

Ask any gym rat and he or she will tell you that there can be no gains unless you are put out of your comfort zone. Remember the saying, "No pain, no gain"? That is as true as it can be.

So dream on, friend! Don't get caught up with your perceived limitations. Think big and work hard to attain those dreams. As you step up the ladder of progress, you will just about find out that the impossible has just become a little bit more possible.

Energy Healing 101: Pranic, Tantric, and Reiki

You have probably come across exotic-sounding terms such as "chakra", "prana", "aura", and "tantra" in your course of reading books on spirituality, sex, and healing in the New Age literature section of the bookstore. But what's the real scoop behind these exotic vocabularies?

Are All Energy Healings the Same?

Chakra or energy center is a term used in Pranic healing, an ancient Hindu system of energy healing. "Prana" means life energy. "Aura" is another terminology traced to Pranic healing. Aura is a non-physical body that consists of energy, which exists along with our physical body. The aura that covers our body is said to have seven layers pertaining to the physical, emotional, mental, and spiritual aspects of an individual as manifested by energy. Studying the color and thickness of auras give ideas on the state of health of individuals. Six colors are associated with aura and interpreted into six personalities. These colors are all present in an individual but one or two are more pronounced.

        Green – ambitious achiever
        Blue – spiritual peacemaker
        White – unconventional chameleon
        Red – activist
        Orange – creative communicator
        Violet - psychic

Although Tantra is popularly associated with the peculiar practice of sex and spirituality, it is another method of energy healing. It comes from the word "tan" which means to spread or expand. The concept of connectedness is a recurring theme in Tantric writings on sex and spirituality. As a method of healing, spirituality and sex figure prominently. It is presupposed that the union of man and woman can reach spiritual levels during orgasm, which removes the body and mind off collected impurities. These impurities being negative energies can in turn manifest as physical illnesses.

Unlike Pranic and Tantric healings, which have Hindu origins, Reiki originated from Japan. It is relatively younger than Pranic and Tantric healings having been rediscovered in the early 1900's. Reiki stands for universal energy, an energy brought forth by higher intelligence. Students of Reiki are taught how to tap this energy to heal physical, emotional, and mental illnesses.

Although Pranic, Tantra, and Reiki are all systems of energy healing, they differ in the type of energy tapped for healing: life energy, sexual energy, and universal energy respectively.

The concepts of the connectedness of mind, body, and spirit; the connection of individuals to all living and nonliving things around them and to the universe; and how energy impacts physical, emotional, and spiritual well-being are some of the salient similarities of these three healing methods.

Why Do People Turn to Energy Healing?

Pranic, Tantric, and Reiki are considered alternative methods of healing. In spite of the availability and relative accessibility of modern medicine, how come more and more people are being drowned to them? Here are some possible reasons:

· Energy healing worked where modern medicine failed.

For several reasons both explainable and explainable, modern medical treatment failed to heal ailments and conditions in several if not many persons. Research or data may not be able to support this statement. But for the families of the dying as well as for the dying patient, they would take the risk of using alternative methods ranging from herbals and organics, faith healers, witch doctors, and New Age healing techniques just to be get well.

· People perceive modern medicine to be isolating.

Medical treatments are oftentimes focused on the disease and its causative agent, which can make a patient feel isolated and treated like a mere host of the disease. Although recent developments in hospital practice are gradually promoting the holistic treatment of a patient, the perception still persists. Unlike in energy healing, since energy and spirituality are intimately linked, the patient feels that all aspects of his health are being attended to.

· Energy healing is non-obtrusive and natural thus it is safer.

Repeated surgical procedures are physically and emotionally traumatic for most patients. It is but a logical and attractive option to both patient and families to look for less stressful health interventions. Moreover, with the rising popularity of New Age religions, going natural is the way to go.

· Energy healing is a good way of relieving stress.

Meditation is part and parcel of energy healing methods and this is an added come-on for highly stressed people. Moreover, sophisticated equipment is not required thus it becomes all the more convenient for students and future students of energy healing.

The battle between alternative healing and mainstream medicine continues as both present the benefits of their approach. But in the final analysis, what matters is the restoration of good health.

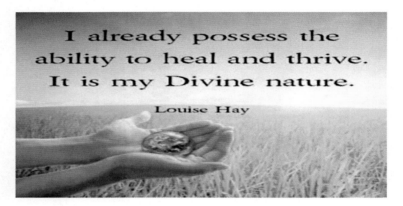

Enjoy Your Life: Change Your Point of View

"Two men look out through the same bars: One sees the mud, and one sees the stars."- Frederick Langbridge, A Cluster of Quiet Thoughts

If you've placed second in a writing contest, will you jump for joy and push for better results the next time or will you be discouraged and find an excuse not to join again?

In life, you are always filled with choices. You may opt to have a pessimist's view and live a self-defeated life or you may decide to take the optimist's route and take a challenging and fulfilling life.

So why nurture an optimist's point of view? And why now?

Well, optimism has been linked to positive mood and good morale; to academic, athletic, military, occupational and political success; to popularity; to good health and even to long life and freedom from trauma.

On the other hand, the rates of depression and pessimism have never been higher. It affects middle-aged adults the same way it hits younger people. The mean age of onset has gone from 30 to 15. It is no longer a middle-aged housewife's disorder but also a teen-ager's disorder' as well.

Here's how optimists are in action and researches that back up why it really pays to be an optimist:

Optimists expect the best

The defining characteristic of pessimists is that they tend to believe bad events, which will last a long time and undermine everything they do, are their own fault.

The truth is optimists are confronted with the same hard knocks of this world. What differs is the way they explain their misfortune---it's the opposite way. They tend to believe defeat is just a temporary setback, that its causes are confined to this one case.

Optimists tend to focus on and plan for the 'problem' at hand. They use 'positive reinterpretation.' In other words, they most likely reinterpret a negative experience in a way that helps them learn and grow. Such people are unfazed by bad situation, they perceive it is a challenge and try harder.

They won't say "things will never get better," "If I failed once, it will happen again" and "If I experience misfortune in one part of my life, then it will happen in my whole life."

Positive expectancies of optimists also predict better reactions during transitions to new environments, sudden tragedies and unlikely turn of events. If they fall, they will stand up. They see opportunities instead of obstacles.

People respond positively to optimists

Optimists are proactive and less dependent on others for their happiness. They find no need to control or manipulate people. They usually draw people towards them. Their optimistic view of the world can be contagious and influence those they are with.

Optimism seems a socially desirable trait in all communities. Those who share optimism are generally accepted while those who spread gloom, panic and hysteria are treated unfavorably.

In life, these people often win elections; get voted most congenial and sought for advice.

When the going gets tough, optimists get tougher

Optimists typically maintain higher levels of subjective well-being during times of stress than do people who are less optimistic. In contrast, pessimists are likely to react to stressful events by denying that they exist or by avoiding dealing with problems. Pessimists are more likely to quit trying when difficulties arise.

They persevere. They just don't give up easily, they are also known for their patience. Inching their way a step closer to that goal or elusive dream.

Optimists are healthier and live longer

Medical research has justified that simple pleasures and a positive outlook can cause a measurable increase in the body's ability to fight disease.

Optimists' health is unusually good. They age well, much freer than most people from the usual physical ills of middle age. And they get to outlive those prone to negative thoughts.

So why not be an optimist today? And think positively towards a more fulfilled life.

Why not look forward to success in all your endeavors? Why not be resilient? Like everybody else you are bound to hit lows sometimes but don't just stay there. Carry yourself out of the mud and improve your chances of getting back on the right track. And why not inspire others to remove their dark-colored glasses and see life in the bright side?

enjoy your own Company

More than One Way to Skin a Cat: Adventures in Creative Thinking

How many times have you caught yourself saying that there could be no other solution to a problem – and that that problem leads to a dead end? How many times have you felt stumped knowing that the problem laying before you is one you cannot solve. No leads. No options. No solutions.

Did it feel like you had exhausted all possible options and yet are still before the mountain – large, unconquerable, and impregnable? When encountering such enormous problems, you may feel like you're hammering against a steel mountain. The pressure of having to solve such a problem may be overwhelming.

But rejoice! There might be some hope yet!

With some creative problem-solving techniques you may be able to look at your problem in a different light. And that light might just be the end of the tunnel that leads to possible solutions.

First of all, in the light of creative problem-solving, you must be open-minded to the fact that there may be more than just one solution to the problem. And, you must be open to the fact that there may be solutions to problems you thought were unsolvable.

Now, with this optimistic mindset, we can try to be a little bit more creative in solving our problems.

Number one; maybe the reason we cannot solve our problems is that we have not really taken a hard look at what the problem is. Here, trying to understanding the problem and having a concrete understanding of its workings is integral solving the problem. If you know how it works, what the problem is, then you have a better foundation towards solving the problem.

Not trying to make the simple statement of what problem is. Try to identify the participating entities and what their relationships with one another are. Take note of the things you stand to gain any stand to lose from the current problem. Now you have a simple statement of what the problem is.
Number two; try to take note of all of the constraints and assumptions you have the words of problem. Sometimes it is these assumptions that obstruct our view of possible solutions. You have to identify which assumptions are valid, in which assumptions need to be addressed.

Number three; try to solve the problem by parts. Solve it going from general view towards the more detailed parts of the problem. This is called the top-down approach. Write down the question, and then come up with a one-sentence solution to that from them. The solution should be a general statement of what will solve the problem. From here you can develop the solution further, and increase its complexity little by little.

Number four; although it helps to have critical thinking aboard as you solve a problem, you must also keep a creative, analytical voice at the back of your head. When someone comes up with a prospective solution, tried to think how you could make that solution work. Try to be creative. At the same time, look for chinks in the armor of that solution.

Number five; it pays to remember that there may be more than just one solution being developed at one time. Try to keep track of all the solutions and their developments. Remember, there may be more than just one solution to the problem.

Number six; remember that old adage," two heads are better than one." That one is truer than it sounds. Always be open to new ideas. You can only benefit from listening to all the ideas each person has. This is especially true when the person you're talking to has had experience solving problems similar to yours.

You don't have to be a gung-ho, solo hero to solve the problem. If you can organize collective thought on the subject, it would be much better.

Number seven; be patient. As long as you persevere, there is always a chance that a solution will present itself. Remember that no one was able to create an invention the first time around.

Creative thinking exercises can also help you in your quest be a more creative problems solver.

Here is one example.
Take a piece of paper and write any word that comes to mind at the center. Now look at that word then write the first two words that come to your mind. This can go on until you can build a tree of related words. This helps you build analogical skills, and fortify your creative processes.

So, next time you see a problem you think you can not solve, think again. The solution might just be staring you right in the face. All it takes is just a little creative thinking, some planning, and a whole lot of work.

"Think Big! Expand your thinking first and your situation will soon follow"
-Loral Langemeier

Spiritual Growth: the Spiritual Challenge of Modern Times

To grow spiritually in a world defined by power, money, and influence is a Herculean task. Modern conveniences such as electronic equipments, gadgets, and tools as well as entertainment through television, magazines, and the web have predisposed us to confine our attention mostly to physical needs and wants. As a result, our concepts of self-worth and self-meaning are muddled. How can we strike a balance between the material and spiritual aspects of our lives?

To grow spiritually is to look inward.

Introspection goes beyond recalling the things that happened in a day, week, or month. You need to look closely and reflect on your thoughts, feelings, beliefs, and motivations. Periodically examining your experiences, the decisions you make, the relationships you have, and the things you engage in provide useful insights on your life goals, on the good traits you must sustain and the bad traits you have to discard. Moreover, it gives you clues on how to act, react, and conduct yourself in the midst of any situation. Like any skill, introspection can be learned; all it takes is the courage and willingness to seek the truths that lie within you. Here are some pointers when you introspect: be objective, be forgiving of yourself, and focus on your areas for improvement.

To grow spiritually is to develop your potentials.

Religion and science have differing views on matters of the human spirit. Religion views people as spiritual beings temporarily living on Earth, while science views the spirit as just one dimension of an individual. Mastery of the self is a recurring theme in both Christian (Western) and Islamic (Eastern) teachings. The needs of the body are recognized but placed under the needs of the spirit. Beliefs, values, morality, rules, experiences, and good works provide the blueprint to ensure the growth of the spiritual being. In Psychology, realizing one's full potential is to self-actualize. Maslow identified several human needs: physiological, security, belongingness, esteem, cognitive, aesthetic, self-actualization, and self-transcendence. James earlier categorized these needs into three: material, emotional, and spiritual. When you have satisfied the basic physiological and emotional needs, spiritual or existential needs come next. Achieving each need leads to the total development of the individual. Perhaps the difference between these two religions and psychology is the end of self-development: Christianity and Islam see that self-development is a means toward serving God, while psychology view that self-development is an end by itself.

To grow spiritually is to search for meaning.

Religions that believe in the existence of God such as Christianism, Judaism, and Islam suppose that the purpose of the human life is to serve the Creator of all things. Several theories in psychology propose that we ultimately give meaning to our lives. Whether we believe that life's meaning is pre-determined or self-directed, to grow in spirit is to realize that we do not merely exist. We do not know the meaning of our lives at birth; but we gain knowledge and wisdom from our interactions with people and from our actions and reactions to the situations we are in. As we discover this meaning, there are certain beliefs and values that we reject and affirm. Our lives have purpose. This purpose puts all our physical, emotional, and intellectual potentials into use; sustains us during trying times; and gives us something to look forward to---a goal to achieve, a destination to reach. A person without purpose or meaning is like a drifting ship at sea.

To grow spiritually is to recognize interconnections.

Religions stress the concept of our relatedness to all creation, live and inanimate. Thus we call other people "brothers and sisters" even if there are no direct blood relations. Moreover, deity-centered religions such as Christianity and Islam speak of the relationship between humans and a higher being. On the other hand, science expounds on our link to other living things through the evolution theory. This relatedness is clearly seen in the concept of ecology, the interaction between living and non-living things. In psychology, connectedness is a characteristic of self-transcendence, the highest human need according to Maslow. Recognizing your connection to all things makes you more humble and respectful of people, animals, plants, and things in nature. It makes you appreciate everything around you. It moves you to go beyond your comfort zone and reach out to other people, and become stewards of all other things around you.

Growth is a process thus to grow in spirit is a day-to-day encounter. We win some, we lose some, but the important thing is that we learn, and from this knowledge, further spiritual growth is made possible.

Does a Law on Human Attraction Exist?

"Opposites attract" is a law of attraction, at least where electromagnetism is concerned. But are there laws about attraction between two people? "In a world that is full of strangers" as a line in a famous song of the 1980's goes, is there a clear set of rules that allows two people to fall for each other?

Is attraction a matter of chemistry?

Maybe. According to scientists, the attraction between animals of the opposite sex is all about chemicals called pheromones. The effect of pheromones in behavior of insects is the most studied to date. It has been observed, at least in some experiments, that pheromones are responsible for communication among same species and colony of ants. The horrible odor released by skunks to ward off enemies is said to be a kind of pheromone. Some species of apes rub pheromone-containing urine on the feet of potential mates to attract them. Some scientists believe that animals (usually the females) such as insects and mammals send out these chemical signals to tell the male of their species that their genes are different from theirs. This gene diversity is important in producing offspring with better chances of survival. The perfume industry has capitalized on pheromones as a means to increase one's sexual attractiveness to the opposite sex. Animals such as the whale and the musk deer were hunted down for these chemicals.

Lately, scientists are looking into the existence of human pheromones and its role in mate selection. There are many conflicting views in the realm of biology, chemistry, genetics, and psychology. Most scientists would assert that these do not exist, or if they do, do not play a role in sexual attraction between a man and a woman. But new researches such as that conducted by Swiss researchers from the University of Bern led by Klaus Wedekind are slowly making these scientists rethink their stand. Their experiment involved women sniffing the cotton shirts of different men during their ovulation period. It was found out that women prefer the smell of men's shirts that were genetically different, but also shared similarities with the women's genes. This, like in the case of insects and other mammals, was to ensure better and healthier characteristics for their future children. But researchers also cautioned that preference for a male odor is affected by the women's ovulation period, the food that men eat, perfumes and other scented body products, and the use of contraceptive pills.

Does personality figure in sexual attraction?

Yes, but so does your perception of a potential mate's personality. According to a research conducted by Klohnen, E.C., & S. Luo in 2003 on interpersonal attraction and personality, a person's sense of self-security and at least the person's perception of his/her partner were found to be strong determinants of attraction in hypothetical situations. What does this tell us? We prefer a certain personality type, which attracts you to a person. But aside from the actual personality of the person, which can only be verified through close interaction through time, it is your perception of your potential partner that attracts you to him/her, whether the person of your affection truly has that kind of personality or not. This could probably account for a statement commonly heard from men and women on their failed relationships: "I thought he/she was this kind of person."

So how does attraction figure in relationships?

You have probably heard that attraction is a prelude, or a factor towards a relationship. Most probably, at least in the beginning; but attraction alone cannot make a relationship work. It is that attraction that makes you notice a person from the opposite sex, but once you get to know the person more, attraction is just one consideration. Shared values, dreams, and passions become more significant in long-term relationships.

So should I stop trying to become attractive?

More than trying to become physically attractive, work on all aspects of your health: physical, emotional, mental, and spiritual. Physical attraction is still a precursor. Remember, biology predisposes us to choose the partner with the healthiest genes. Where your emotions are concerned, just ask this to yourself: would you want to spend time with a person who feels insecure about him/herself? Probably not! There is wisdom in knowing yourself: who you are, your beliefs, values, and dreams. And do not pretend to be someone you are not. Fooling another person by making him/her think that you share the same values and beliefs is only going to cause you both disappointments. When you are healthy in all aspects, attractiveness becomes a consequence and not an end. As mentioned in the Klohnen and Luo's research, a person's sense of self-security matters, perhaps even beyond attraction. But remember: do these things for yourself and not for other people. Only then can you truly harness your attractiveness as a person.

Genuine Happiness Comes from Within

Life isn't the sweetest candy. Sometimes, when I feel like the world is just too heavy, I look around and find people who continued to live fascinating and wonderful lives. And then thoughts come popping into my mind like bubbles from nowhere – "How did their life become so adorably sweet? How come they still can manage to laugh and play around despite a busy stressful life?" Then I pause and observed for awhile... I figured out that maybe, they start to work on a place called 'self'.

So, how does one become genuinely happy? Step 1 is to love yourself.

My theology professor once said that "loving means accepting." To love oneself means to accept that you are not a perfect being, but behind the imperfections must lie a great ounce of courage to be able to discover ways on how to improve your repertoire to recover from our mistakes.

Genuine happiness also pertains to contentment. When you are contented with the job you have, the way you look, with your family, your friends, the place you live in, your car, and all the things you now have – truly, you know the answer to the question "how to be genuinely happy."

When we discover a small start somewhere from within, that small start will eventually lead to something else, and to something else. But if you keep questioning life lit it has never done you any good, you will never be able to find genuine happiness.

I believe that life is about finding out about right and wrong, trying and failing, wining and losing. These are things that happen as often as you inhale and exhale. Failure, in a person's life has become as abundant and necessary as air. But this should not hinder us from becoming happy.

How to be genuinely happy in spite all these? I tell you... every time you exert effort to improve the quality of life and your being, whether it is cleaning up your room, helping a friend, taking care of your sick dog, fail on board exams and trying again, life gives you equivalent points for that.

Imagine life as a big score board like those which are used in the NFLs. Every time you take a step forward, you make scoring points. Wouldn't it be nice to look at that board at the end of each game and think to yourself "Whew! I got a point today. I'm glad I gave it a shot.", instead of looking at it all blank and murmur "Geez, I didn't even hit a score today. I wish I had the guts to try out. We could have won!" and then walk away.

Genuine happiness isn't about driving the hottest Formula 1 car, nor getting the employee of the year award, earning the highest 13th month pay, or beating the sales quota. Sometimes, the most sought after prizes in life doesn't always go to the fastest, the strongest, the bravest or not even the best. So, how do you become genuinely happy? Every one has his own definition of 'happiness'. Happiness for a writer may mean launching as much best selling books as possible. Happiness for a basketball rookie may mean getting the rookie of the year award. Happiness for a beggar may mean a lot of money. Happiness for a business man may mean success. So, really now, how do we become genuinely happy? Simple. You don't have to have the best things in this world. Its about doing and making the best out of every single thing. When you find yourself smiling at your own mistake and telling your self "Oh, I'll do better next time", you carry with you a flame of strong will power to persevere that may spread out like a brush fire. You possess a willingness to stand up again and try – that will make you a genuinely happy person.

When you learn to accept yourself and your own faults. You pass step 1 in the project "how to become genuinely happy".For as long as you know how to accept others, you will also be accepted. For as long as you love and know how to love, you will receive love ten folds back.

Again, throw me that same question "how to become genuinely happy?". I'll refer you to a friend of mine who strongly quoted- "Most of us know that laughter is the best medicine to life's aches and pain. But most of us don't know that the best kind of laughter is laughter over self. Coz then you don't just become happy... you become free."

"The Way to Wellness" It's time to start a Healthy life: your 7 days program

How many times have you gone to sleep at night, swearing you'll go to the gym in the morning, and then changing your mind just eight hours later because when you get up, you don't feel like exercising?

While this can happen to the best of us, it doesn't mean you should drop the ball altogether when it comes to staying fit. What people need to realize is that staying active and eating right are critical for long-term health and wellness -- and that an ounce of prevention is worth a pound of cure. The more you know about how your body responds to your lifestyle choices, the better you can customize a nutrition and exercise plan that is right for you. When you eat well, increase your level of physical activity, and exercise at the proper intensity, you are informing your body that you want to burn a substantial amount of fuel. This translates to burning fat more efficiently for energy.
In other words, proper eating habits plus exercise equals fast metabolism, which, in turn gives you more energy throughout the day and allows you to do more physical work with less effort.

The true purpose of exercise is to send a repetitive message to the body asking for improvement in metabolism, strength, aerobic capacity and overall fitness and health. Each time you exercise, your body responds by upgrading its capabilities to burn fat throughout the day and night, Exercise doesn't have to be intense to work for you, but it does need to be consistent.

I recommend engaging in regular cardiovascular exercise four times per week for 20 to 30 minutes per session, and resistance training four times per week for 20 to 25 minutes per session. This balanced approach provides a one-two punch, incorporating aerobic exercise to burn fat and deliver more oxygen, and resistance training to increase lean body mass and burn more calories around the block.

Here's a sample exercise program that may work for you:

* Warm Up -- seven to eight minutes of light aerobic activity intended to increase blood flow and lubricate and warm-up your tendons and joints.

* Resistance Training -- Train all major muscle groups. One to two sets of each exercise. Rest 45 seconds between sets.

* Aerobic Exercise -- Pick two favorite activities, they could be jogging, rowing, biking or cross-country skiing, whatever fits your lifestyle. Perform 12 to 15 minutes of the first activity and continue with 10 minutes of the second activity. Cool down during the last five minutes.

* Stretching -- Wrap up your exercise session by stretching, breathing deeply, relaxing and meditating.

When starting an exercise program, it is important to have realistic expectations. Depending on your initial fitness level, you should expect the following changes early on.

* From one to eight weeks -- Feel better and have more energy.

* From two to six months -- Lose size and inches while becoming leaner. Clothes begin to fit more loosely. You are gaining muscle and losing fat.

* After six months -- Start losing weight quite rapidly.

Once you make the commitment to exercise several times a week, don't stop there. You should also change your diet and/or eating habits,' says Zwiefel. Counting calories or calculating grams and percentages for certain nutrients is impractical. Instead, I suggest these easy-to-follow guidelines:

* Eat several small meals (optimally four) and a couple of small snacks throughout the day
* Make sure every meal is balanced -- incorporate palm-sized proteins like lean meats, fish, egg whites and dairy products, fist-sized portions of complex carbohydrates like whole-wheat bread and pasta, wild rice, multigrain cereal and potatoes, and fist-sized portions of vegetable and fruits
* Limit your fat intake to only what's necessary for adequate flavor
* Drink at least eight 8-oz. glasses of water throughout the day
* I also recommend that you take a multi-vitamin each day to ensure you are getting all the vitamins and minerals your body needs.

How to Become an Ideal Leader

When you are at work, do you get frustrated because things don't seem to be happening the way they're supposed to be? You see people milling around but nothing gets accomplished. And in the daily hustle and bustle, do you feel that your goals remain just that – goals. Then maybe its time for you to stand up and do something about it.

Most people are content just to stand around listening for orders. And it isn't unusual to adopt a follow-the-leader mentality. But maybe, somewhere inside of you, you feel the desire to make things happen – to be the head, not the tail. Then maybe leadership just suits you fine.

Some people believe that great leaders are made, not born. Yes, it may be true that some people are born with natural talents. However, without practice, without drive, without enthusiasm, and without experience, there can be no true development in leadership.

You must also remember that good leaders are continually working and studying to improve their natural skills. This takes a commitment to constantly improve in whatever endeavor a person chooses.

First of all, let's define leadership. To be a leader, one must be able to influence others to accomplish a goal, or an objective. He contributes to the organization and cohesion of a group.

Contrary to what most people believe, leadership is not about power. It is not about harassing people or driving them using fear. It is about encouraging others towards the goal of the organization. It is putting everyone on the same page and helping them see the big picture of the organization. You must be a leader not a boss.

First of all, you have to get people to follow you. How is this accomplished?

People follow others when they see a clear sense of purpose. People will only follow you if they see that you know where you are going. Remember that bumper sticker? The one that says, don't follow me, I'm lost too? The same holds true for leadership. If you yourself do not know where you're headed to, chances are people will not follow you at all.
You yourself must know the vision of the organization. Having a clear sense of hierarchy, knowing who the bosses are, who to talk to, the organization's goals and objectives, and how the organization works is the only way to show others you know what you are doing.

Being a leader is not about what you make others do. It's about who you are, what you know, and what you do. You are a reflection of what you're subordinates must be.

Studies have shown that one other bases of good leadership is the trust and confidence your subordinates have of you. If they trust you they will go through hell and high water for you and for the organization.

Trust and confidence is built on good relationships, trustworthiness, and high ethics.

The way you deal with your people, and the relationships you build will lay the foundation for the strength of your group. The stronger your relationship, the stronger their trust and confidence is in your capabilities.

Once you have their trust and confidence, you may now proceed to communicate the goals and objectives you are to undertake.

Communication is a very important key to good leadership. Without this you can not be a good leader. The knowledge and technical expertise you have must be clearly imparted to other people.

Also, you can not be a good leader and unless you have good judgment. You must be able to assess situations, weigh the pros and cons of any decision, and actively seek out a solution.

It is this judgment that your subordinates will come to rely upon. Therefore, good decision-making is vital to the success of your organization.

Leaders are not do-it-all heroes. You should not claim to know everything, and you should not rely upon your skills alone.
You should recognize and take advantage of the skills and talents your subordinates have. Only when you come to this realization will you be able to work as one cohesive unit.

Remember being a leader takes a good deal of work and time. It is not learned overnight. Remember, also, that it is not about just you. It is about you and the people around you.

So, do you have the drive and the desire to serve required of leaders? Do you have the desire to work cooperatively with other people? Then start now. Take your stand and be leader today.

Do Yoda Proud: Meditation 101

Meditation refers to a state where your body and mind are consciously relaxed and focused. Practitioners of this art report increased awareness, focus, and concentration, as well as a more positive outlook in life.

Meditation is most commonly associated with monks, mystics and other spiritual disciplines. However, you don't have to be a monk or mystic to enjoy its benefits. And you don't even have to be in a special place to practice it. You could even try it in your own living room!

Although there are many different approaches to meditation, the fundamental principles remain the same. The most important among these principles is that of removing obstructive, negative, and wandering thoughts and fantasies, and calming the mind with a deep sense of focus. This clears the mind of debris and prepares it for a higher quality of activity.

The negative thoughts you have – those of noisy neighbors, bossy officemates, that parking ticket you got, and unwanted spam– are said to contribute to the 'polluting' of the mind, and shutting them out is allows for the 'cleansing' of the mind so that it may focus on deeper, more meaningful thoughts.

Some practitioners even shut out all sensory input – no sights, no sounds, and nothing to touch – and try to detach themselves from the commotion around them. You may now focus on a deep, profound thought if this is your goal. It may seem deafening at first, since we are all too accustomed to constantly hearing and seeing things, but as you continue this exercise you will find yourself becoming more aware of everything around you.

If you find the meditating positions you see on television threatening – those with impossibly arched backs, and painful-looking contortions – you need not worry. The principle here is to be in a comfortable position conducive to concentration. This may be while sitting cross-legged, standing, lying down, and even walking.

If the position allows you to relax and focus, then that would be a good starting point. While sitting or standing, the back should be straight, but not tense or tight. In other positions, the only no-no is slouching and falling asleep.
Loose, comfortable clothes help a lot in the process since tight fitting clothes have a tendency to choke you up and make you feel tense.

The place you perform meditation should have a soothing atmosphere. It may be in your living room, or bedroom, or any place that you feel comfortable in. You might want an exercise mat if you plan to take on the more challenging positions (if you feel more focused doing so, and if the contortionist in you is screaming for release). You may want to have the place arranged so that it is soothing to your senses.

Silence helps most people relax and meditate, so you may want a quiet, isolated area far from the ringing of the phone or the humming of the washing machine. Pleasing scents also help in that regard, so stocking up on aromatic candles isn't such a bad idea either.

The monks you see on television making those monotonous sounds are actually performing their mantra. This, in simple terms, is a short creed, a simple sound which, for these practitioners, holds a mystic value.

You do not need to perform such; however, it would pay to note that focusing on repeated actions such as breathing, and humming help the practitioner enter a higher state of consciousness.

The principle here is focus. You could also try focusing on a certain object or thought, or even, while keeping your eyes open, focus on a single sight.

One sample routine would be to – while in a meditative state – silently name every part of you body and focusing your consciousness on that part. While doing this you should be aware of any tension on any part of your body. Mentally visualize releasing this tension. It works wonders.

In all, meditation is a relatively risk-free practice and its benefits are well worth the effort (or non-effort – remember we're relaxing).

Studies have shown that meditation does bring about beneficial physiologic effects to the body. And there has been a growing consensus in the medical community to further study the effects of such. So in the near future, who knows, that mystical, esoteric thing we call meditation might become a science itself!

Motivation, the heart of self improvement

Pain may sometimes be the reason why people change. Getting flunked grades make us realize that we need to study. Debts remind us of our inability to look for a source of income. Being humiliated gives us the 'push' to speak up and fight for ourselves to save our face from the next embarrassments. It may be a bitter experience, a friend's tragic story, a great movie, or an inspiring book that will help us get up and get just the right amount of motivation we need in order to improve ourselves.

With the countless negativities the world brings about, how do we keep motivated? Try on the tips I prepared from A to Z…

A - Achieve your dreams. Avoid negative people, things and places. Eleanor Roosevelt once said, "the future belongs to those who believe in the beauty of their dreams."

B - Believe in your self, and in what you can do.

C – Consider things on every angle and aspect. Motivation comes from determination. To be able to understand life, you should feel the sun from both sides.

D – Don't give up and don't give in. Thomas Edison failed once, twice, more than thrice before he came up with his invention and perfected the incandescent light bulb. Make motivation as your steering wheel.

E – Enjoy. Work as if you don't need money. Dance as if nobody's watching. Love as if you never cried. Learn as if you'll live forever. Motivation takes place when people are happy.

F – Family and Friends – are life's greatest 'F' treasures. Don't loose sight of them.

G – Give more than what is enough. Where does motivation and self improvement take place at work? At home? At school? When you exert extra effort in doing things.

H – Hang on to your dreams. They may dangle in there for a moment, but these little stars will be your driving force.

I – Ignore those who try to destroy you. Don't let other people to get the best of you. Stay out of toxic people – the kind of friends who hates to hear about your success.

J – Just be yourself. The key to success is to be yourself. And the key to failure is to try to please everyone.

K – keep trying no matter how hard life may seem. When a person is motivated, eventually he sees a harsh life finally clearing out, paving the way to self improvement.
L – Learn to love your self. Now isn't that easy?

M – Make things happen. Motivation is when your dreams are put into work clothes.

N – Never lie, cheat or steal. Always play a fair game.

O – Open your eyes. People should learn the horse attitude and horse sense. They see things in 2 ways – how they want things to be, and how they should be.

P – Practice makes perfect. Practice is about motivation. It lets us learn repertoire and ways on how can we recover from our mistakes.

Q – Quitters never win. And winners never quit. So, choose your fate – are you going to be a quitter? Or a winner?

R – Ready yourself. Motivation is also about preparation. We must hear the little voice within us telling us to get started before others will get on their feet and try to push us around. Remember, it wasn't raining when Noah build the ark.

S – Stop procrastinating.

T – Take control of your life. Discipline or self control jives synonymously with motivation. Both are key factors in self improvement.

U – Understand others. If you know very well how to talk, you should also learn how to listen. Yearn to understand first, and to be understood the second.

V – Visualize it. Motivation without vision is like a boat on a dry land.

W – Want it more than anything. Dreaming means believing. And to believe is something that is rooted out from the roots of motivation and self improvement.

X – X Factor is what will make you different from the others. When you are motivated, you tend to put on "extras" on your life like extra time for family, extra help at work, extra care for friends, and so on.

Y – You are unique. No one in this world looks, acts, or talks like you. Value your life and existence, because you're just going to spend it once.

Z – Zero in on your dreams and go for it!!!

You're recommended Daily Allowance for Relaxation

Stress is the curse of living in modern times. Everyone suffers from stress. And the stress we suffer takes a heavy toll on our bodies, emotions and minds.

Feeling stressed out, worn out by fatigue or just simply having a miserable day, the best thing to do is relax.

Watching television may be a form of relaxation for some, but is not a recommended method by experts. When we watch TV we are bombarded with commercials, ads, sounds and images. So how do we achieve relaxation? If there are thousands of ways we can get stressed, one of them is not meeting deadlines, there are also many ways we can relax.

In recent studies, experts have determined that heart disease is linked to anger and irritability is linked to mental stress. Too much stress brings about ischemia that can lead to or cause a heart attack. Relaxation takes on added importance in light of this matter. Managing your anger and attitude is significant to heart health, and relaxation can help you manage stress.

One way of relaxation is transcendental meditation. Recent studies have also shown that this method might reduce artery blockage, which is a major cause for heart attack and stroke. People practice transcendental meditation by repeating uttering soothing sounds while meditating, this is to achieve total relaxation. The researchers found that practitioners of transcendental meditation significantly reduced the thickness of their arterial wall compared with those who didn't practice transcendental meditation.

Another study on another method of relaxation, acupuncture, seems to reduce high blood pressure by initiating several body functions for the brain to release chemical compounds known as endorphins. Endorphin helps to relax muscles, ease panic, decrease pain, and reduce anxiety.

Yoga is also another method for relaxation and may also have similar effects like acupuncture. In another study, participants were subjected to several minutes of mental stress. Then they were subjected to various relaxation techniques, such as listening to nature sounds or classical music. Only those who did Yoga significantly reduced the time it took for their blood pressures to go back to normal. Yoga is a form of progressive relaxation.
Breathing is one of the easiest methods to relax. Breathing influences alamost all aspects of us, it affects our mind, our moods and our body. Simply focus on your breathing, after some time you can feel its effects right away.

There are several breathing techniques that can help you reduce stress.

Another easy way to achieve relaxation is exercise. If you feel irritated a simple half-hour of exercise will often settle things down. Although exercise is a great way to lose weight, it does not show you how to manage stress appropriately. Exercise should also be used in conjunction with other exercise method.

One great way of relaxation is getting a massage. To gain full relaxation, you need to totally surrender to the handling and touch of a professional therapist.

There are several types of massages that also give different levels of relaxation.

Another method of relaxation is Biofeedback. The usual biofeedback-training program includes a 10-hour sessions that is often spaced one week apart.

Hypnosis is one controversial relaxation technique. It is a good alternative for people who think that they have no idea what it feels like to be relaxed. It is also a good alternative for people with stress related health problems.

Drugs are extreme alternatives to relaxation. They are sometimes not safe and are not effective like the other relaxation methods. This method is only used by trained medical professionals on their patients.

These relaxation techniques are just some of the ways you can achieve relaxation. Another reason why we need to relax, aside from lowering blood pressure in people and decreasing the chances of a stroke or a heart attack, is because stress produces hormones that suppress the immune system, relaxation gives the immune system time to recover and in doing so function more efficiently.
Relaxation lowers the activities within the brains' limbic system; this is the emotional center of our brain.

Furthermore, the brain has a periodic need for a more pronounced activity on the right-hemisphere. Relaxation is one way of achieving this.

Relaxation can really be of good use once a relaxation technique is regularly built into your lifestyle. Choose a technique that you believe you can do regularly.

No one in the world was ever you before, with your particular gifts and abilities and possibilities.

JOSEPH CAMPBELL

WWW.**VERYBESTQUOTES**.COM

The Powers of a Positive Attitude

I am going to ask you to something very weird right now. First of all, I want you to listen to your thoughts. Now tell me, what thoughts fill your head? Would you label them as positive, or negative?

Now let's say you are walking down the street with these thoughts. Do you think anyone who would meet you would be able to tell you what's on your mind?

The answer to number one is up to you. But, the answer number two can be pretty generic. Although people will not be able to tell you exactly what you think, they will more or less have an idea of how you are feeling.

Here's another question. When you enter a party filled with friends, do they all fall silent as if something terrible had happened? Or does everybody there perk up as if waiting for something exciting to happen?

You know what? The answer to all these depends on your frame of mind.

Thoughts are very powerful. They affect your general attitude. The attitude you carry reflects on your appearance, too – unless, of course, you are a great actor.

And it doesn't end there. Your attitude can also affect people around you.

The type of attitude you carry depends on you. It can be either positive or negative.

Positive thoughts have a filling effect. They are admittedly invigorating. Plus, the people around the person carrying positive thoughts are usually energized by this type of attitude.

Negative thoughts on the other hand have a sapping effect on other people. Aside from making you look gloomy and sad, negative thoughts can turn a festive gathering into a funeral wake.

A positive attitude attracts people, while a negative attitude repels them. People tend to shy away from those who carry a negative attitude.

We can also define attitude as the way of looking at the world. If you choose to focus on the negative things in the world, more or less you have a negative attitude brewing up. However, if you choose to focus on the positive things, you are more likely carry a positive attitude.

You have much to gain from a very positive attitude. For one, studies have shown that a positive attitude promotes better health. Those with this kind of attitude also have more friends. projecting a positive attitude also helps one to handle stress and problems better than those who have a negative attitude.

A positive attitude begins with a healthy self-image. If you will love the way you are and are satisfied, confident, and self-assured, you also make others are around feel the same way.

A negative attitude, on the other hand, has, of course, an opposite effect. So, carrying a negative attitude has a twofold drawback. You feel bad about yourself, and you make others feel the same way.

If you want to have a positive attitude, you have to feature healthy thoughts. This is probably very hard to do nowadays since, all around us, the media feeds us nothing but negative thoughts. A study shows that for every 14 things a parent says to his or her child, only one is positive. This is truly a saddening thought.

If you want a healthier outlook in life, you need to think happy thoughts, and you have to hear positive things as well. So, what can you do? Well, for starters, you could see a funny movie, you could play with children, spend some time telling jokes with friends. All these activities fill you with positive stimuli, which in turn promotes positive attitude.

Although it is impossible to keep ourselves from the negative things around us, you can still carry a positive attitude by focusing on the good things, the positive things in life.

And this positive attitude you now carry can be of benefit to other people. Sometimes when other people feel down, the thing people mostly do is try to give them advice. But sometimes, all they need is somebody to sit by them, and listen to them. If you have a positive attitude you may be able to cheer them up without even having to say anything.

If positive attitude is really great, why do people choose to adopt a negative attitude instead? One who carries a negative attitude may be actually sending a signal for attention. Before you get me wrong, feeling sad, angry, or gloomy is not wrong itself. But dwelling on these thoughts for far too long is not healthy either. There is a time to mourn.

As always, if you are beset by troubles, even in your darkest hour, focus on the good things in life, you will always have hope. Problems become something you can overcome.

You do not have much to lose by adopting a healthy, positive attitude. Studies show that such an attitude actually retards aging, makes you healthier, helps you develop a better stress coping mechanism, and has a very positive effect on all the people you meet every day. So, what's not to like about a positive attitude? Adopt one today.

One small positive thought in the morning can change your whole day

Power through the people

Have you come across a person who is so naturally friendly that when you put him inside a room of strangers, he'll be friends with almost everyone in no time? We call such a people-person, someone unbelievably nice and charismatic that he can charm anyone into doing anything.

A socially-empowered person achieves so much greatness, basically because of the people that catapult him to success. He earns the trust and all-out support of the people, whom he had helped before. He never runs out of help. He can do anything with the plethora of people behind him. All because he knows he maximizes his social potential!

See, if you know your social skills and you make use of them, you will reach self-empowerment. Self-empowerment is making a general overhaul in your life and turning yourself into a happier and more successful person. If you can be one of those people-persons, then I can't see any reason why you will not succeed. You just have to know how to start.

1. Be genuine.

Hypocrisy will just bring you all the way down. Be genuinely nice and interested to people. Once they perceive that you are Mr. Hypocrite with selfish intentions, you might as well say goodbye to self-empowerment.

2. Be the greatest listener that you can be.

To earn the love and trust of the people, listen to their problems and sympathize with them. Do not just hear them out, listen to them with your heart. Make eye contact when the person talks to you. Listen as if every word matters, and it does. Brownie points when they find out that there is a confidante in you.

3. Laugh out loud.

I do not mean that you force yourself to laugh for every joke cracked by someone, albeit you do not find it funny at all. This means finding humor in things and not being too darn serious. A person oozing with an awesome sense of humor attracts crowds and eventually, attracts success.

4. Don't forget yourself.

In the process of fluttering around like a social butterfly, you might forget yourself, allowing everyone to push you over. Remember, love and value yourself before anyone else. If you deem yourself respectable and worthy of affection, people will flock to you and not trample on you.

5. Do random acts of kindness.

You don't have to do a John Rockefeller and blow your savings to charity. Little acts of kindness matters the most, and this can be as simple as giving someone a surprise you-take-care card or helping an elderly cross the street. When we were kindergarten students, kindness was taught to us and greatly practiced. Now is the time to revive the good deeds and this time, let them stay for good.

6. Contact your old friends.

Sad how some friendships are destined to goodbye, but thanks to technology, you can do something about it. Relive the good old days by flipping your yearbook and look for the great people whom you want to communicate with again. Adding these old friends to your roster of support peers will surely make you feel good all over.

7. Develop your personality.

Are you grouchy, grumpy and generally morose? Whoa, you can't go through life with those. Get rid of the bad traits and habits that perpetually hamper your growth. And really, who wants a grouchy friend anyway?
8. Be confident.

Be able to stride to the other corner of the room and introduce yourself to people with that winning smile of yours. Just remember: be confident, not arrogant.

9. Practice control.

When angry, don't snap at anyone. Never throw a tantrum. Stay calm and collected. Be adult enough to take control of situation and transform your anger into something more productive and passive. As soon as people think your anger goes to volcanic proportions easily, they will find it hard to come to you.

10. Keep nurturing your relationships.

Your relationship with your family, friends and significant others is too precious that you must not neglect it whatever happens. Go out and have fun with them. Do things together. Happiness will never fly from your side as long as the people who matter the most are close to you.

In the end, using people for self-empowerment means becoming a better and more lovable person. It's a win-win situation: the people know they can turn to you anytime and vice versa.

We don't meet people by accident. They are meant to cross our path for a Reason.

Self improvement and success

Everything that happens to us happens in purpose. And sometimes, one thing leads to another. Instead of locking yourself up in your cage of fears and crying over past heartaches, embarrassment and failures, treat them as your teachers and they will become your tools in both self improvement and success.

I remember watching Patch Adams – its my favorite movie, actually. Its one great film that will help you improve yourself. Hunter "patch" Adams is a medical student who failed to make it through the board exams. After months of suffering in melancholy, depression and suicidal attempts – he decided to seek for medical attention and voluntarily admitted himself in a psychiatric ward. His months of stay in the hospital led him to meeting different kinds of people. Sick people in that matter. He met a catatonic, a mentally retarded, a schizophrenic and so on. Patch found ways of treating his own ailment and finally realized he has to get back on track. He woke up one morning realizing that after all the failure and pains he has gone through, he still want to become the a doctor. He carries with himself a positive attitude that brought him self improvement and success. He didn't only improved himself, but also the life of the people around him and the quality of life. Did he succeed? Needless to say, he became the best damn doctor his country has ever known.

So, when does self improvement become synonymous with success? Where do we start? Take these tips, friends…
*Stop thinking and feeling as if you're a failure, because you're not. How can others accept you if YOU can't accept YOU?

*When you see hunks and models on TV, think more on self improvement, not self pitying. Self acceptance is not just about having nice slender legs, or great abs. Concentrate on inner beauty.

*When people feel so down and low about themselves, help them move up. Don't go down with them. They'll pull you down further and both of you will end up feeling inferior.

*The world is a large room for lessons, not mistakes. Don't feel stupid and doomed forever just because you failed on a science quiz. There's always a next time. Make rooms for self improvement.
*Take things one at a time. You don't expect black sheep's to be goody-two-shoes in just a snap of a finger. Self improvement is a one day at a time process.

*Self improvement results to inner stability, personality development and dig this …. SUCCESS. It comes from self confidence, self appreciation and self esteem.

* Set meaningful and achievable goals. Self improvement doesn't turn you to be the exact replica of Cameron Diaz or Ralph Fiennes. It hopes and aims to result to an improved and better YOU.

*Little things mean BIG to other people. Sometimes, we don't realize that the little things that we do like a pat on the back, saying "hi" or "hello", greeting someone "good day" or telling Mr. Smith something like "hey, I love your tie!" are simple things that mean so much to other people. When we're being appreciative about beautiful things around us and other people, we also become beautiful to them.

*When you're willing to accept change and go through the process of self improvement, it doesn't mean that everyone else is. The world is a place where people of different values and attitude hang out. Sometimes, even if you think you and your best friend always like to do the same thing together at the same time, she would most likely decline an invitation for self improvement.

We should always remember that there's no such thing as 'over night success'. Its always a wonderful feeling to hold on to the things that you already have now, realizing that those are just one of the things you once wished for. A very nice quote says that "When the student is ready, the teacher will appear." We are all here to learn our lessons. Our parents, school teachers, friends, colleagues, officemates, neighbors… they are our teachers. When we open our doors for self improvement, we increase our chances to head to the road of success.

Life is About Choices and the Decisions We Make

Life is like a road. There are long and short roads; smooth and rocky roads; crooked and straight paths. In our life many roads would come our way as we journey through life. There are roads that lead to a life of single blessedness, marriage, and religious vocation. There are also roads that lead to fame and fortune on one hand, or isolation and poverty on the other. There are roads to happiness as there are roads to sadness, roads towards victory and jubilation, and roads leading to defeat and disappointment.

Just like any road, there are corners, detours, and crossroads in life. Perhaps the most perplexing road that you would encounter is a crossroad. With four roads to choose from and with limited knowledge on where they would go, which road will you take? What is the guarantee that we would choose the right one along the way? Would you take any road, or just stay where you are: in front of a crossroad?

There are no guarantees.

You do not really know where a road will lead you until you take it. There are no guarantees. This is one of the most important things you need to realize about life. Nobody said that choosing to do the right thing all the time would always lead you to happiness. Loving someone with all your heart does not guarantee that it would be returned. Gaining fame and fortune does not guarantee happiness. Accepting a good word from an influential superior to cut your trip short up the career ladder is not always bad, especially if you are highly qualified and competent. There are too many possible outcomes, which your really cannot control. The only thing you have power over is the decisions that you will make, and how you would act and react to different situations.

Wrong decisions are always at hindsight.

Had you known that you were making a wrong decision, would you have gone along with it? Perhaps not, why would you choose a certain path when you know it would get you lost? Why make a certain decision if you knew from the very beginning that it is not the right one. It is only after you have made a decision and reflected on it that you realize its soundness. If the consequences or outcomes are good for you, then you have decided correctly. Otherwise, your decision was wrong.

Take the risk: decide.

Since life offers no guarantee and you would never know that your decision would be wrong until you have made it, then you might as well take the risk and decide. It is definitely better than keeping yourself in limbo. Although it is true that one wrong turn could get you lost, it could also be that such a turn could be an opportunity for an adventure, moreover open more roads. It is all a matter of perspective. You have the choice between being a lost traveller or an accidental tourist of life. But take caution that you do not make decisions haphazardly. Taking risks is not about being careless and stupid. Here are some pointers that could help you choose the best option in the face of life's crossroads:

Get as many information as you can about your situation.

You cannot find the confidence to decide when you know so little about what you are faced with. Just like any news reporter, ask the 5 W's: what, who, when, where, and why. What is the situation? Who are the people involved? When did this happen? Where is this leading? Why are you in this situation? These are just some of the possible questions to ask to know more about your situation. This is important. Oftentimes, the reason for indecision is the lack of information about a situation.

· Identify and create options.

What options do the situation give you? Sometimes the options are few, but sometimes they are numerous. But what do you do when you think that the situation offers no options? This is the time that you create your own. Make your creative mind work. From the most simplistic to the most complicated, entertain all ideas. Do not shoot anything down when an idea comes to your head. Sometimes the most outrageous idea could prove to be the right one in the end. You can ask a friend to help you identify options and even make more options if you encounter some difficulty, but make sure that you make the decision yourself in the end.

· Weigh the pros and cons of every option.

Assess each option by looking at the advantages and disadvantages it offers you. In this way, you get more insights about the consequences of such an option.

· Trust yourself and make that decision.

Now that you have assessed your options, it is now time to trust yourself. Remember that there are no guarantees and wrong decisions are always at hindsight. So choose... decide... believe that you are choosing the best option at this point in time.

Now that you have made a decision, be ready to face its consequences: good and bad. It may take you to a place of promise or to a land of problems. But the important thing is that you have chosen to live your life instead of remaining a bystander or a passive audience to your own life. Whether it is the right decision or not, only time can tell. But do not regret it whatever the outcome. Instead, learn from it and remember that you always have the chance to make better decisions in the future.

Setting Your Goals - Easier Said, Easily Done

The basics of setting a goal is an open secret known by top-caliber athletes, successful businessmen and businesswomen and all types of achievers in all the different fields. The basics of setting goals give you short-term and long-term motivation and focus. They help you set focus on the acquisition of required knowledge and help you to plan and organize your resources and your time so that you can get the best out of your life.

Setting clearly defined short term and long term goals will enable you to measure your progress and achieve personal satisfaction once you have successfully met your goals. Charting your progress will also enable you to actually see the stages of completion leading to the actual realization of your goals. This eliminates the feeling of a long and pointless grind towards achieving your goal. Your self-confidence and level of competence will also improve as you will be more aware of your capabilities as you complete or achieve your goals.

The basics of goal settings will involve deciding what you really want to do with your personal life and what short term and long term goals you need to achieve it. Then you have to break down goals into the smaller and manageable targets that you must complete in your way to achieving your lifetime targets. Once you have your list waste no time in tackling your goals.

A good way to have a manageable list is to have a daily and weekly set of goals. By doing this you will be always in the position of going towards you life plan goals. Everyday will give you the opportunity to fulfill a certain goal giving you the feeling of accomplishment.

Here are some pointers that should be taken into consideration in setting goals and achieving them.

Attitude plays a very big role in setting and achieving your goals. You must ask yourself if any part of you or your mind holding you back towards completing your simplest goals? If there are any part of your behavior that is being a hindrance or puts your plans into disarray? If you do have problems in these areas then the immediate thing to do is to address this problem. Solutions may include a visit to a doctor or psychiatrist to control your emotions.

Careers are made by good time management practice. Failing in a career is often attributed to bad time management. Careers require a lot from an individual which often makes the career the life of the individual. Plan how far do you want to go into your career.

Education is key in achieving your goals. If your goals require you to have a certain kind of degree or require a certain specialization or demand a certain skill to be developed, make plans in getting the appropriate education.

Your family should never be left out of your plans. If you are just starting out then you have to decide if you want to be a parent or when you want to be a parent. You also have to know if you really would be a good parent and how well would you relate to extended family members

Personal financial situations also play a major role in achieving your goals. Have a realistic goal on how much you really want to earn. You also must be able to create plans or stages by which you will be able to reach your earning potential.

Physically gifted individuals may be able to achieve sports related goals like being in the National Basketball association or National Football League. Determining your physical capabilities should be one of your priorities. Physical limitations could however be conquered with proper planning.

As the saying goes -'All work and no play makes Jack a dull boy', or something to that effect, is by all means true down to the last the letter. Giving yourself a little pleasure: should be included into your plans.

To start achieving your lifetime goals, set a quarter of a century plan, then break it down to 5 year plans then break it down again to 1 year plans, then 6 month plans then monthly plans, then weekly, then daily.

Then create a things-to-do list for the day.

Always review your plans and prepare for contingencies.

The basics of goal settings should not be so difficult once you get to be familiar with them.

Creative Notions

People seem to have the misconception that only a select few are able to unleash a steady flow of creative genius. That is not true at all. The fact is, creativity is very much like a muscle that needs to be exercised in order to consistently give out great results. If you don't practice harnessing creative thinking, this skill will very much atrophy into inexistence. But keep working and this skill will soon come to you in a snap.

So how do you unleash your creative thinking? Well, the first thing is to become a human leech. No, we're not talking about just sucking the blood out of every living being available, we're saying that you should take in as much knowledge and learning you can find. Read everything available -- good and bad, and keep your mind open to the infinite possibilities of the universe. The more you know, the more you'll want to know, and the more your faculty of wonder will be exercised. Prepare to be amazed at little facts that add a bit of color into your life.

Focus on a creative activity everyday. Yes, it's an effort. Even doodling is a creative activity. Don't let anything hinder you. Mindlessness may be a creative activity, but for people who are just starting out to unleash a little bit of creative thinking in their lives, it is helpful and encouraging to have concrete evidence, that, "hey, what I'm doing is getting somewhere." So why don't you try it. Practice drawing for a couple of minutes each day. Bring out your old camera and start snapping photos like crazy. Keep a journal and make a point to write in it religiously. Another cool idea is to write by describing something with your five senses. Try to avoid vague adjectives like "marvelous," "amazing," and "delicious." Before you know it, you'll have built yourself a tiny portfolio, and you'll be amazed at the growth you've undertaken after amassing all those works of art. Who knows, you might actually take to liking those things you do everyday. Pretty soon those things will become a part of you and you'll be addicted to these creative exercises.

Think out of the box -- or don't. Sometimes, constraints are actually a good thing. Limitations discipline you to work within your means. It enables you to be more resourceful. Creative freedom is great, but limitations enforce discipline.

Try something new everyday and let your experiences broaden your perspective. Explore a new district in your neighborhood. Spend an afternoon in a museum to which you've never been before. Chat up someone on the bus. Open up to the people around you. As you thrust yourself out of your comfort zone more and more each day, your sense of adventure grows and so does your zest for life. Think about it. When was the last time you did something for the first time? If it's been a while, I tell you, you've been missing out on a whole lot of experiences that could've added to your growth, emotionally, mentally, physically, or spiritually. Why don't you try bungee jumping today? Not only will you learn, but you will also have plenty of stories to share, enabling you to practice your storytelling skills and making you the life of the party.

Embrace insanity. No, not to the point of practically admitting yourself into the mental ward. As John Russell once said, "Sanity calms, but madness is more interesting." Exactly! Every creative thought was once deemed insanity by other "normal" people at one time or another. Luckily, that didn't stop the creative geniuses from standing by them. The thing is, sanity or being normal confines people to think... well, normally.

Withink limits. Creativity is essentially breaking through barriers. Yes, this includes the bizarre and the downright strange. I'm not saying that you yourself should develop a creative personality. That might go haywire. An example of a creative personality would be George Washington, who often rode into battle naked, or James Joyce, who wrote "Dubliners" with beetle juice for an intense fear of ink, or Albert Einstein, who thought his cat was a spy sent by his rival (or in thinking creatively in this case, the term could probably be "archnemesis.") It's important that your creativity doesn't get you detached from the real world completely.

The Key to a Better Life

Time management is basically about being focused. The Pareto Principle also known as the '80:20 Rule' states that 80% of efforts that are not time managed or unfocused generates only 20% of the desired output. However, 80% of the desired output can be generated using only 20% of a well time managed effort. Although the ratio '80:20' is only arbitrary, it is used to put emphasis on how much is lost or how much can be gained with time management.

Some people view time management as a list of rules that involves scheduling of appointments, goal settings, thorough planning, creating things to do lists and prioritizing. These are the core basics of time management that should be understood to develop an efficient personal time management skill. These basic skills can be fine tuned further to include the finer points of each skill that can give you that extra reserve to make the results you desire.

But there is more skills involved in time management than the core basics. Skills such as decision making, inherent abilities such as emotional intelligence and critical thinking are also essential to your personal growth.

Personal time management involves everything you do. No matter how big and no matter how small, everything counts. Each new knowledge you acquire, each new advice you consider, each new skill you develop should be taken into consideration.

Having a balanced life-style should be the key result in having personal time management. This is the main aspect that many practitioners of personal time management fail to grasp.

Time management is about getting results, not about being busy.

The six areas that personal time management seeks to improve in anyone's life are physical, intellectual, social, career, emotional and spiritual.

The physical aspect involves having a healthy body, less stress and fatigue.
The intellectual aspect involves learning and other mental growth activities.

The social aspect involves developing personal or intimate relations and being an active contributor to society.

The career aspect involves school and work.

The emotional aspect involves appropriate feelings and desires and manifesting them.

The spiritual aspect involves a personal quest for meaning.

Thoroughly planning and having a set of things to do list for each of the key areas may not be very practical, but determining which area in your life is not being giving enough attention is part of time management. Each area creates the whole you, if you are ignoring one area then you are ignoring an important part of yourself.

Personal time management should not be so daunting a task. It is a very sensible and reasonable approach in solving problems big or small.

A great way of learning time management and improving your personal life is to follow several basic activities.

One of them is to review your goals whether it be immediate or long-term goals often.

A way to do this is to keep a list that is always accessible to you.

Always determine which task is necessary or not necessary in achieving your goals and which activities are helping you maintain a balanced life style.

Each and everyone of us has a peek time and a time when we slow down, these are our natural cycles. We should be able to tell when to do the difficult tasks when we are the sharpest.

Learning to say "No". You actually see this advice often. Heed it even if it involves saying the word to family or friends.

Pat yourself at the back or just reward yourself in any manner for an effective time management result.

Try and get the cooperation from people around you who are actually benefiting from your efforts of time management.

Don't procrastinate. Attend to necessary things immediately.

Have a positive attitude and set yourself up for success. But be realistic in your approach in achieving your goals.

Have a record or journal of all your activities. This will help you get things in their proper perspective.

These are the few steps you initially take in becoming a well rounded individual.

As the say personal time management is the art and science of building a better life.

From the moment you integrate into your life time management skills, you have opened several options that can provide a broad spectrum of solutions to your personal growth. It also creates more doors for opportunities to knock on.

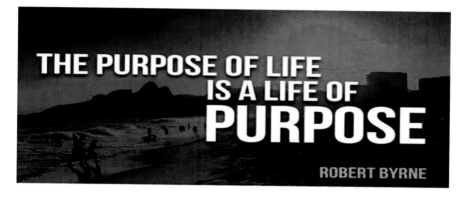

Leadership Exposed: Things You Thought You Knew About Leadership

Much has been written about leadership: rules, pointers, styles, and biographies of inspiring leaders throughout world history. But there are certain leadership ideas that we ourselves fail to recognize and realize in the course of reading books. Here is a short list of things you thought you knew about leadership.

1. Leaders come in different flavors.

There are different types of leaders and you will probably encounter more than one type in your lifetime. Formal leaders are those we elect into positions or offices such as the senators, congressmen, and presidents of the local clubs. Informal leaders or those we look up to by virtue of their wisdom and experience such as in the case of the elders of a tribe, or our grandparents; or by virtue of their expertise and contribution on a given field such as Albert Einstein in the field of Theoretical Physics and Leonardo da Vinci in the field of the Arts. Both formal and informal leaders practice a combination of leadership styles.

· Lewin's three basic leadership styles – authoritative, participative, and delegative
· Likert's four leadership styles – exploitive authoritative, benevolent authoritative, consultative, and participative
· Goleman's six emotional leadership styles - visionary, coaching, affiliative, democratic, pacesetting, and commanding.

2. Leadership is a process of becoming.

Although certain people seem to be born with innate leadership qualities, without the right environment and exposure, they may fail to develop their full potential. So like learning how to ride a bicycle, you can also learn how to become a leader and hone your leadership abilities. Knowledge on leadership theories and skills may be formally gained by enrolling in leadership seminars, workshops, and conferences. Daily interactions with people provide the opportunity to observe and practice leadership theories. Together, formal and informal learning will help you gain leadership attitudes, gain leadership insights, and thus furthering the cycle of learning. You do not become a leader in one day and just stop. Life-long learning is important in becoming a good leader for each day brings new experiences that put your knowledge, skills, and attitude to a test.

3. Leadership starts with you.

The best way to develop leadership qualities is to apply it to your own life. As an adage goes "action speaks louder than words." Leaders are always in the limelight. Keep in mind that your credibility as a leader depends much on your actions: your interaction with your family, friends, and co-workers; your way of managing your personal and organizational responsibilities; and even the way you talk with the newspaper vendor across the street. Repeated actions become habits. Habits in turn form a person's character. Steven Covey's book entitled 7 Habits of Highly Effective People provides good insights on how you can achieve personal leadership.

4. Leadership is shared.

Leadership is not the sole responsibility of one person, but rather a shared responsibility among members of an emerging team. A leader belongs to a group. Each member has responsibilities to fulfill. Formal leadership positions are merely added responsibilities aside from their responsibilities as members of the team. Effective leadership requires members to do their share of work. Starting as a mere group of individuals, members and leaders work towards the formation of an effective team. In this light, social interaction plays a major role in leadership. To learn how to work together requires a great deal of trust between and among leaders and members of an emerging team. Trust is built upon actions and not merely on words. When mutual respect exists, trust is fostered and confidence is built.

5. Leadership styles depend on the situation.

How come dictatorship works for Singapore but not in the United States of America? Aside from culture, beliefs, value system, and form of government, the current situation of a nation also affects the leadership styles used by its formal leaders. There is no rule that only one style can be used. Most of the time, leaders employ a combination of leadership styles depending on the situation. In emergency situations such as periods of war and calamity, decision-making is a matter of life and death. Thus, a nation's leader cannot afford to consult with all departments to arrive at crucial decisions. The case is of course different in times of peace and order---different sectors and other branches of government can freely interact and participate in governance. Another case in point is in leading organizations. When the staffs are highly motivated and competent, a combination of high delegative and moderate participative styles of leadership is most appropriate. But if the staffs have low competence and low commitment, a combination of high coaching, high supporting, and high directing behavior from organizational leaders is required.

Now that you are reminded of these things, keep in mind that there are always ideas that we think we already know; concepts we take for granted, but are actually the most useful insights on leadership.

"Relaxing with a Mental PDA" Your 5 minutes daily program to Stress management

We all have this favorite expression when it comes to being stressed out, and I wouldn't bother naming all of them since it may also vary in different languages. But when it comes down to it, I think that it is how we work or even relax, for that matter that triggers stress. Ever been stressed even when you're well relaxed and bored? I know I have.

Since Error! Hyperlink reference not valid. is unavoidable in life, it is important to find ways to decrease and prevent stressful incidents and decrease negative reactions to stress. Here are some of the things that can be done by just remembering it, since life is basically a routine to follow like brushing your teeth or eating breakfast. You can do a few of them in a longer span of time, but as they say-- every minute counts.

Managing time

Time management skills can allow you more time with your family and friends and possibly increase your performance and productivity. This will help reduce your stress.

To improve your time management:

· Save time by focusing and concentrating, delegating, and scheduling time for yourself.
· Keep a record of how you spend your time, including work, family, and leisure time.
· Prioritize your time by rating tasks by importance and urgency. Redirect your time to those activities that are important and meaningful to you.
· Manage your commitments by not over- or undercommitting. Don't commit to what is not important to you.
· Deal with procrastination by using a day planner, breaking large projects into smaller ones, and setting short-term deadlines.
· Examine your beliefs to reduce conflict between what you believe and what your life is like.
Build healthy coping strategies

It is important that you identify your coping strategies. One way to do this is by recording the stressful event, your reaction, and how you cope in a stress journal. With this information, you can work to change unhealthy coping strategies into healthy ones-those that help you focus on the positive and what you can change or control in your life.

Lifestyle

Some behaviors and lifestyle choices affect your stress level. They may not cause stress directly, but they can interfere with the ways your body seeks relief from stress. Try to:

· Balance personal, work, and family needs and obligations.
· Have a sense of purpose in life.
· Get enough sleep, since your body recovers from the stresses of the day while you are sleeping.

· Eat a balanced diet for a nutritional defense against stress.
· Get moderate exercise throughout the week.
· Limit your consumption of alcohol.
· Don't smoke.

Social support

Social support is a major factor in how we experience stress. Social support is the positive support you receive from family, friends, and the community. It is the knowledge that you are cared for, loved, esteemed, and valued. More and more research indicates a strong relationship between social support and better mental and physical health.

Changing thinking

When an event triggers negative thoughts, you may experience fear, insecurity, anxiety, depression, rage, guilt, and a sense of worthlessness or powerlessness. These emotions trigger the body's stress, just as an actual threat does. Dealing with your negative thoughts and how you see things can help reduce stress.

· Thought-stopping helps you stop a negative thought to help eliminate stress.
· Disproving irrational thoughts helps you to avoid exaggerating the negative thought, anticipating the worst, and interpreting an event incorrectly.
· Problem solving helps you identify all aspects of a stressful event and find ways to deal with it.
· Changing your communication style helps you communicate in a way that makes your views known without making others feel put down, hostile, or intimidated. This reduces the stress that comes from poor communication. Use the assertiveness ladder to improve your communication style.

Even writers like me can get stressed even though we're just using our hands to do the talking, but having to sit for 7 or 8 hours is already stressful enough and have our own way to relieve stress. Whether you're the mail guy, the CEO, or probably the average working parent, stress is one unwanted visitor you would love to boot out of your homes, especially your life.

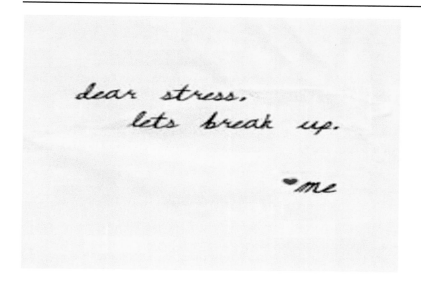

"Enlightenment" Your 7 days program to Positive thinking

I'm sure you have a bright idea hidden somewhere in the back of your mind that you just can't wait to test out. Of course you're not the only one with the bright idea. So what motivates you to churn those creative, or even inspiring juices to its utmost flavor?

It's always best to set up a personal goal where you can accomplish the most in record time, maybe like mowing the lawn in an hour before the big game on TV. A correct and positive attitude in whatever you do will make things easier, and even enjoyable.

Here are some tips to make it through the week even if you're just sitting in your favorite couch. An idea takes time to form in your head and is always at work while you are busy sitting.

Having a bit of positive thinking can help you realize things that are never thought possible. Thinking big is indeed the American Way and that what made our country prosperous.

1. Take passionate action towards living your life by design. Talk is cheap. Action = deposits in the bank of a passionately authentic future. Without it, passion is void.

This is a perfect example where dreams are made of where you start by tinkering with your mind, then with your hands. And if the idea weakens, you can always go back to it later until you finish it.

2. Commit to yourself as well as those you love to create powerfully a life you can love. Instead of reacting, commit to creating from your heart and soul, out of love rather than fear. The American Dream will always be there, but a dream will still be a dream without motion. Be amazed as the transformation begins.

3. Recognize and embrace the thought that each moment is perfect regardless of its outcome. Every time you hit on something that may appear too extreme, why not give it a shot and see if it will work. You will be surprised to see of there are other ways to get the task done in time. If you are not pleased with the outcome, decide to use that moment to learn from and make the appropriate shift.

4. Dwell completely in a place of gratitude. Learn to utilize what you have in your hands and make use of it in the most constructive way. Slipping into neediness will become less of a habit when you repeatedly shift towards gratitude, away from poverty consciousness.

5. Use a Passion Formula of Recognize/Reevaluate/Restore in place of the Shoulda/Woulda/Coulda whirlwind. The former is based in increased knowledge and abundance while the latter focuses on scarcity and lack. As you face people or tasks that may seem harder than scaling the summit of the Himalayas, allow yourself to realize that the task is just as important as giving out orders to your subordinates. You would rather be richly passionate!

6. Keep humor at the forefront of thought, laughing at and with yourself when possible. You may find yourself quite entertaining when you loosen up! I am yet to see a comedian ever go hungry even though his jokes are as 'old as great-grandma'. Life has so much to offer to allow you to mope around in self pity. Humor is very attractive, very passionate: life-giving.

7. Believe that you are the architect of your destiny. No one can take your passionate future from you except for you! Create your life authentically. As long as there's still breath in your body, there is no end to how much you can accomplish in a lifetime. The concept of thinking big is all about enjoying your work, which would lead to celebrate a discovery that is born within your hands. Watch everything flow into place with perfect, passionate precision.

It's interesting how people get wallowed up by something trivial as learning to use a computer, when nowadays that top computer companies are manufacturing software that even the kids can do it. I don't mean to be condescending, but that's the idea of not having any positive thinking in your life-you'll just end up as a dim bulb in a dark corner. So instead of subjecting yourself to what you will be doomed for, make your path by taking the first step with a positive attitude.

Life Mapping: A Vision of Success

Success is more than economic gains, titles, and degrees. Planning for success is about mapping out all the aspects of your life. Similar to a map, you need to define the following details: origin, destination, vehicle, backpack, landmarks, and route.

Origin: Who you are

A map has a starting point. Your origin is who you are right now. Most people when asked to introduce themselves would say, "Hi, I'm Jean and I am a 17-year old, senior highschool student." It does not tell you about who Jean is; it only tells you her present preoccupation. To gain insights about yourself, you need to look closely at your beliefs, values, and principles aside from your economic, professional, cultural, and civil status. Moreover, you can also reflect on your experiences to give you insights on your good and not-so-good traits, skills, knowledge, strengths, and weaknesses. Upon introspection, Jean realized that she was highly motivated, generous, service-oriented, but impatient. Her inclination was in the biological-medical field. Furthermore, she believed that life must serve a purpose, and that wars were destructive to human dignity.

Destination: A vision of who you want to be

"Who do want to be?" this is your vision. Now it is important that you know yourself so that you would have a clearer idea of who you want to be; and the things you want to change whether they are attitudes, habits, or points of view. If you hardly know yourself, then your vision and targets for the future would also be unclear. Your destination should cover all the aspects of your being: the physical, emotional, intellectual, and spiritual. Continuing Jean's story, after she defined her beliefs, values, and principles in life, she decided that she wanted to have a life dedicated in serving her fellowmen.

Vehicle: Your Mission

A vehicle is the means by which you can reach your destination. It can be analogized to your mission or vocation in life. To a great extent, your mission would depend on what you know about yourself. Bases on Jean's self-assessment, she decided that she was suited to become a doctor, and that she wanted to become one. Her chosen vocation was a medical doctor. Describing her vision-mission fully: it was to live a life dedicated to serving her fellowmen as a doctor in conflict-areas.

Travel Bag: Your knowledge, skills, and attitude

Food, drinks, medicines, and other travelling necessities are contained in a bag. Applying this concept to your life map, you also bring with you certain knowledge, skills, and attitudes. These determine your competence and help you in attaining your vision. Given such, there is a need for you to assess what knowledge, skills, and attitudes you have at present and what you need to gain along the way. This two-fold assessment will give you insights on your landmarks or measures of success. Jean realized that she needed to gain professional knowledge and skills on medicine so that she could become a doctor. She knew that she was a bit impatient with people so she realized that this was something she wanted to change.

Landmarks and Route: S.M.A.R.T. objectives

Landmarks confirm if you are on the right track while the route determines the travel time. Thus, in planning out your life, you also need to have landmarks and a route. These landmarks are your measures of success. These measures must be specific, measurable, attainable, realistic, and time bound. Thus you cannot set two major landmarks such as earning a master's degree and a doctorate degree within a period of three years, since the minimum number of years to complete a master's degree is two years. Going back to Jean as an example, she identified the following landmarks in her life map: completing a bachelor's degree in biology by the age of 21; completing medicine by the age of 27; earning her specialization in infectious diseases by the age of 30; getting deployed in local public hospitals of their town by the age of 32; and serving as doctor in war-torn areas by the age of 35.

Anticipate Turns, Detours, and Potholes

The purpose of your life map is to minimize hasty and spur-of-the-moment decisions that can make you lose your way. But oftentimes our plans are modified along the way due to some inconveniences, delays, and other situations beyond our control. Like in any path, there are turns, detours, and potholes thus; we must anticipate them and adjust accordingly.

Contact

Titus Maduwa

Millionaire Pillars™, World Class Trading Secrets®
P.O. Box 782284 Sandton | Johannesburg | Gauteng |
2146 | South Africa| Email:
tradingsecrets@millionairepillars.co.za or
info@millionairepillars.co.za Call: +27 84 667 1524

Limits of Liability and Disclaimer of Warranty
The author and publisher shall not be liable for your misuse of this material. This book is strictly
for informational and educational purposes.

Warning – Disclaimer
The purpose of this book is to educate and entertain. The author and/or publisher do not
guarantee that anyone following these techniques, suggestions, tips, ideas, or strategies will
become successful. The author and/or publisher shall have neither liability nor responsibility to

anyone with respect to any loss or damage caused, or alleged to be caused, directly or indirectly by the information contained in this book.

LEGAL NOTICE:

The Publisher has strived to be as accurate and complete as possible in the creation of this little book, notwithstanding the fact that he does not warrant or represent at any time that the contents within are accurate due to the rapidly changing nature of the Internet.

While all attempts have been made to verify information provided in this publication, the Publisher assumes no responsibility for errors, omissions, or contrary interpretation of the subject matter herein. Any perceived slights of specific persons, peoples, or organizations are unintentional.

In practical advice books, like anything else in life, there are no guarantees of income made. Readers are cautioned to reply on their own judgment about their individual circumstances to act accordingly.

This book is not intended for use as a source of legal, business, accounting or financial advice. All readers are advised to seek services of competent professionals in legal, business, accounting, and finance field.

You are encouraged to print this book for easy reading.

About The Information Inside World Class Trading

See What Others Are Saying About The Information Inside World Class Trading Secrets

" Mr.T you really know how to inspire people. I pray every day to GOD so that he gives you more days in this world you mean a lot to our life.God bless." - Lawrence Mathiane...

When You enroll in The World Class Trading Secrets Coaching Program, you'll learn how to:

-How to double your profits in both ways-Create a crystal clear vision for the kind of Trading Financial Markets you'll like to have that suits your personality style-Trade 24x5 from home or anywhere-Determine your own position size-You will also learn how to utilize the art of leverage/Trade on margin that will give you the ability to make nice profits-Articulate trading strategies so you can connect with your currency market and make the trend flow fall in love with you-Add entry points,Trail stops set target limits and to instantly increase your profits as well on your trading account-Create an irresistible trades alerts to signal you before you place a trade-Set up trades charts studies and endorsed drawings to get 10x exposure of quality trend flow and 10x profits- AND Much,much MORE.......

A Power House Support

One on One Coaching with Titus Maduwa- You will also have access to our private World Class Trading Secrets Skype,WeChat, WhatsApp group coupled with our Facebook community where you will be sharing some experiences with other pro traders

When you register today you'll get access to........

- 4 Step-by-Step in depth coaching modules,over 7 hours of pure trading producing content that will have you giddy with excitement because you can taste your future success....and it's ALL taught by Titus Maduwa- A professionally designed World Class Trading Secrets in printable PDF format for jotting down all key points,biggest learning's and powerful trading exercises- A Special bonus digital recording on how to plant the right seed for success and mindset readiness taught by Titus Maduwa.

What Others Are Saying About The Information Inside World Class Trading Secrets....

" I absolutely loved this program. The coaching segments presented by Titus Maduwa really offer the clearest,most practically useful street-smart advice on trading as a professional career i have ever heard. Thanks." -Monyane Ramaphiri

Made in the USA
Middletown, DE
06 February 2023

24147978R00073